MONTANA BEFORE HISTORY

11,000 Years of Hunter-Gatherers
in the Rockies and Plains

MONTANA BEFORE HISTORY

*11,000 Years of Hunter-Gatherers
in the Rockies and Plains*

Douglas H. MacDonald

2012
Mountain Press Publishing Company
Missoula, Montana

Cover art and title page art by Eric Carlson

Photos © 2012 by Douglas H. MacDonald unless otherwise credited

Illustrations © 2012 by Douglas H. MacDonald unless otherwise credited

Library of Congress Cataloging-in-Publication Data

MacDonald, Douglas H., 1968-
 Montana before history : 11,000 years of hunter-gatherers in the
Rockies and Great Plains / Douglas H. MacDonald.
     p. cm.
 Includes bibliographical references and index.
 ISBN 978-0-87842-585-3 (pbk. : alk. paper)
 1. Paleo-Indians—Montana. 2. Hunting and gathering societies—
Montana. 3. Montana—Antiquities. I. Title.
 E78.M9M34 2012
 978.6'01—dc23
                              2011046449

Printed in Hong Kong

MP Mountain Press
PUBLISHING COMPANY
P.O. Box 2399 • Missoula, MT 59806 • 406-728-1900
800-234-5308 • info@mtnpress.com
www.mountain-press.com

Acknowledgments

This book owes thanks to many students who have taken Anthropology 352 (the Archaeology of Montana) at the University of Montana in Missoula over the last few years. These students complained so much about the high cost and antiquity of the only available textbook on the topic that I finally got around to writing my own book to use in class. The main goal of the book is to provide an introduction to the prehistory of Montana and surrounding areas. While this book won't exhaust you with details, I hope it will prepare you to dig deeper into the early human history of Montana.

This book would not have been possible without the support of my wife (Amy Keil), her parents (Otto and Carol), and my children (Molly and Otto), as well as my parents (Richard and Patricia MacDonald). Thanks also to the Department of Anthropology at the University of Montana for providing me with a wonderful opportunity to become a member of the Montana archaeological community. Many members of that community—including many members of the Montana Archaeological Society—have been helpful in the last few years, including Ann Johnson, Elaine Hale, and Tobin Roop of Yellowstone National Park; Lon Johnson of Glacier National Park; Mark Baumler, Stan Wilmoth, and Damon Murdo of the Montana Historical Society; Christine Whitacre and Pei-Lin Yu of the National Park Service; Doug Melton, Maria Craig, and Jason Strahl of the Bureau of Land Management; Carl Davis, Walt Allen, Milo McLeod, Justin Moschelle, and Ed DeCleva of the U.S. Forest Service; Weber Greiser and Todd Ahlman of HRA; Sara Scott of Montana Fish, Wildlife and Parks; Scott Carpenter; Larry Lahren; Ruthann Knudson; Lynelle Peterson of Ethnoscience; Mavis and John Greer; Steve Platt of the Montana Department of Transportation; Matt Root of Rainshadow Research; and Leslie Davis, Jack Fisher, and Tom Roll of Montana State University. Many of these individuals also provided images for use in this book. Jordan McIntyre and Jennifer Carey produced the maps, while Eric Carlson illustrated many of the figures.

I hope you enjoy reading this book and come away from it with a better grasp of how and where the hunter-gatherers of Montana lived. Hundreds of archaeologists have excavated thousands of sites in Montana, collecting tidbits of information that have become the basis for this book. My final thanks is to them for their years of hard digging and troweling in the sand, clay, and silt of Montana and the surrounding region.

Contents

Period		Years ago*	Points/ Culture	Significant Events	Key Sites in Montana
Late Prehistoric		300 1,000	small points Avonlea	Introduction of horse in 1700s first permanent villages First use of bow and arrow	Hagen Ulm Pishkun
Archaic	**Late Plains**	2,000 3,000	Besant Pelican Lake	Emergence of Great Plains bison hunting culture	Wahkpa Chu'gn
	Middle Plains	4,000 5,000	Oxbow and McKean	Period of transition back to bison hunting	Sun River
	Early Plains	6,000 7,000 8,000	large side-notched	First pit houses *Bison antiquus* goes extinct First definitive use of atlatl with side-notched point Altithermal, period of hot, dry climate, occurs between 8,000 and 5,000 years ago	Buckeye Myers-Hindman
Paleoindian	**Late**	9,000 10,000	Cody Agate Basin/ Hell Gap	Intensive bison hunting Increased use of uplands	Mammoth Meadow Barton Gulch KXGN-TV
	Early	11,000 12,000	Folsom Goshen Clovis	First bison hunters Cooling climate coincides with extinctions of megafauna First people in Montana People on west coast of North America	MacHaffie Mill Iron Anzick

(Foothill/Mountain — spanning Late Paleoindian points Cody and Agate Basin/Hell Gap)

* Based on uncalibrated radiocarbon dates

The Hunter-Gatherers of Montana

For most of the past 11,000 years, people living in Montana have been hunter-gatherers, obtaining food by hunting and foraging instead of growing crops and raising animals. In most states, the switch to agriculture began 2,000 years ago. However, hunter-gatherers in Montana maintained their traditional way of life until European-American contact in the eighteenth and nineteenth centuries. From the collection of chokecherry and camas root to the hunting of pronghorn, sheep, and bison to the procurement of obsidian, chert, and basalt for toolmaking, Montana's first people were extremely knowledgeable about their natural environment.

Montana Before History describes the human inhabitants of Montana during the last 11,000 years, from the Clovis people of the Paleoindian period to the Native Americans of the Late Prehistoric period prior to European-American contact. In order to reconstruct the chronology of human occupation in the state, I present the archaeological data from major sites in Montana. The book explores the prehistory of Montana within the broader context of the surrounding Great Plains, Columbia Plateau, and Rocky Mountains and thus also includes important information from archaeological sites and projects in Wyoming, North Dakota, South Dakota, and Idaho, as well as the adjacent Canadian provinces of British Columbia, Alberta, and Saskatchewan. Hunter-gatherers were mobile people, so the story of Montana's prehistoric people is not complete without including their region of travel and influence.

In this book I use the standard human chronology for the northwestern Great Plains established by George C. Frison of the University of Wyoming and used by many Great Plains archaeologists. The periods of human occupation are as follows:

Paleoindian: 11,000 to 8,000 years ago

Early Plains Archaic: 8,000 to 5,000 years ago

Middle Plains Archaic: 5,000 to 3,000 years ago

Late Plains Archaic: 3,000 to 1,500 years ago

Late Prehistoric: 1,500 to 300 years ago

Historical: 300 years ago to present time

1

Other cultural chronologies are available for Montana, including the Early, Middle, and Late Prehistoric period chronology established by William Mulloy in 1958 for his research at Pictograph Cave near Billings. Alan McMillan and Eldon Yellowhorn also proposed a useful Early Dog Days and Late Dog Days chronology for the prehistory of the nearby Canadian Plains. Frison's model is the most widely accepted by Great Plains archaeologists, so I use it here. Artifacts found at archaeological sites, especially projectile points and pottery, help identify the period the site was used.

Hunters of the Clovis Culture were arguably the first people to arrive in Montana, approximately 11,000 years ago during the Paleoindian period. It is uncertain where they came from, whether from the north, west, south, or east. They hunted mammoths and other large animals with fluted spear points until those animals suddenly disappeared approximately 10,900 years ago.

CALIBRATED AND UNCALIBRATED RADIOCARBON DATES

Archaeologists can determine the age of charcoal in fire pits, bones, and plant remains by measuring how much radioactive carbon 14 has decayed since the death of the organism. I won't go into the complexity of this analysis here, but it is important to understand the distinction between calibrated and uncalibrated radiocarbon dates. In the description of the chronology of human history in Montana, I use uncalibrated radiocarbon years before present. Calibrated radiocarbon dates can be nearly 2,000 years older than uncalibrated dates, increasing in divergence with age. For example, the Mill Iron Site in eastern Montana dates to approximately 10,900 uncalibrated years ago; when this date is calibrated, it becomes approximately 12,800 years ago. The calibration takes into account environmental fluctuations that affect radiocarbon decay rates, increasing their accuracy. In recent years some archaeologists have switched to the use of calibrated dates. However, given that much of the archaeological research in Montana occurred prior to the use of calibrated dates and the fact that calibrations change frequently with updated data, I have maintained the traditional use of uncalibrated dates in this book. When comparing information in this book to other sources, be sure to check whether such sources use calibrated or uncalibrated dates.

Montana hunter-gatherers adapted to climatic cooling between 10,800 and 10,200 years ago by hunting bison and other remaining game. They elaborated upon their Clovis fluted spear points to produce Folsom points—among the most exquisite projectile points ever produced by humans. After Folsom came a series of Late Paleoindian cultures—Agate Basin/Hell Gap and Cody—that embraced bison hunting as the staple of subsistence until about 8,000 years ago. These cultures hunted with stemmed spear points attached to either spears or atlatls.

During the Early Plains Archaic period, hunter-gatherers of Montana experienced a hot, dry climate called the Altithermal, which occurred between approximately 8,000 and 5,000 years ago. *Bison antiquus*, the target of choice for Paleoindian hunters, became extinct due to dramatic climate change. A smaller species, *Bison bison*, emerged. The Early Plains

SITE NAMES

In this book I refer to archaeological sites by their accepted names or by the official state designation. Newly identified archaeological sites are named after either the site discoverer or the property owner. For example, the Anzick Site in Wilsall, Montana—a site that dates to 11,040 years ago—is named after the landowner. The RJP-1 Site in Yellowstone National Park near Gardiner, Montana, is named with the initials of the site discoverer (one of my students) Robert J. Peltier, with the numeral 1 indicating it as the first site Peltier found during our fieldwork in the summer of 2008.

In addition to personal site names, each site is given an official state number by the State Historic Preservation Office. In Montana, the preservation office is part of the Montana Historical Society. Whenever a new site is identified in the state, the site discoverer completes an official archaeological site form, assigns the site a personal site name, and submits the form to the preservation office, where the site is assigned a unique state number. The official site number for the Anzick Site in Wilsall is 24PA506. The first number, *24*, is the Montana state number. (All Montana site numbers begin with 24.) *PA* stands for Park County, and *506* marks it as the 506th site identified in Park County. When discussing an important site, I typically call it by its personal name. An appendix lists all sites discussed in the book, organized by state. Official site numbers are provided for most of them.

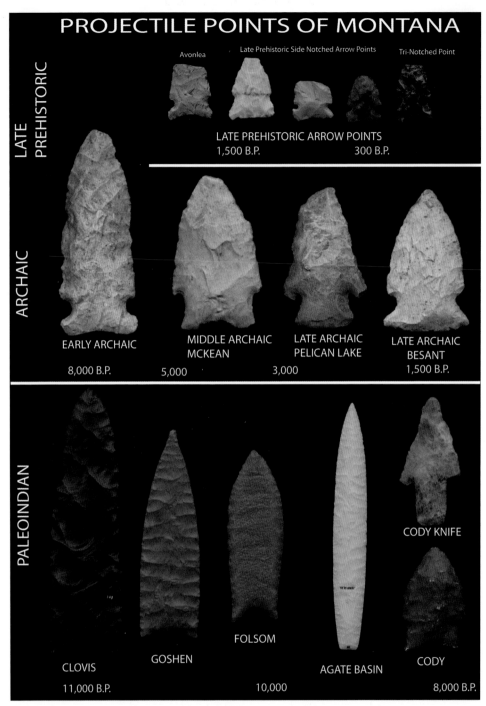

PROJECTILE POINTS OF MONTANA

LATE PREHISTORIC

Avonlea   Late Prehistoric Side Notched Arrow Points   Tri-Notched Point

LATE PREHISTORIC ARROW POINTS
1,500 B.P.   300 B.P.

ARCHAIC

EARLY ARCHAIC

MIDDLE ARCHAIC
MCKEAN

LATE ARCHAIC
PELICAN LAKE

LATE ARCHAIC
BESANT

8,000 B.P.   5,000   3,000   1,500 B.P.

PALEOINDIAN

CODY KNIFE

FOLSOM

GOSHEN

CLOVIS

AGATE BASIN

CODY

11,000 B.P.   10,000   8,000 B.P.

Projectile points are some of the main artifacts used to identify cultures and the periods in which they lived. During the Paleoindian period, large elaborate points were used with spears and possibly atlatls. Projectile point technology changed over the course of the Archaic period, with the use of large side-notched points in the Early Archaic, bifurcate points during the Middle Archaic, and smaller side- and corner-notched points in the Late Archaic, all used with atlatls. During the Late Prehistoric, smaller points were used on arrows. The Clovis point measures approximately 14 centimeters long. B.P. means "before present."

Archaic period was an anomaly in the prehistory of Montana, one of the few eras in which bison hunting seems to have been abandoned in favor of other fauna. Early Archaic hunters utilized side-notched projectile points attached to dart tips that were thrown with atlatls.

Between 5,000 and 3,000 years ago, during the Middle Plains Archaic period, bison gradually returned as the preferred prey of Great Plains hunter-gatherers east of the Continental Divide, while diversified subsistence continued in the Rocky Mountains and west of the Continental Divide. Middle Plains Archaic hunters utilized Oxbow and McKean bifurcate projectile points.

During the Late Plains Archaic period, from 3,000 to 1,500 years ago, bison hunting became the dominant subsistence pattern for Great Plains peoples. They used bison jumps and corrals all over the northwestern Great Plains and Rocky Mountains and left behind evidence of their campsites: stone circles that mark the initial use of tepees in Montana. Late Plains Archaic people used Pelican Lake and Besant projectile points and were also engaged in widespread trade with cultures from the east and west. As a testament to this, Knife River Flint from North Dakota and obsidian from Yellowstone National Park have been found in archaeological sites dating to the Late Plains Archaic period in Ohio, Pennsylvania, and Michigan, among other states.

The Late Prehistoric period, from 1,500 to 300 years ago, marks the climax of Great Plains bison hunting cultures in Montana east of the Continental Divide. West of the Divide, hunter-gatherers hunted deer, elk, and sheep, fished for trout, and collected wild roots. They also ventured east of the Rockies to hunt large herds of bison. The use of buffalo jumps was extremely popular during the time just before European-American contact. Several hundred bison jump sites have been recorded in Montana alone, most dating to the Late Prehistoric period. This period also marks the beginning of the use of the bow and arrow in Montana, prior to which use of the atlatl, or spear thrower, was widespread. Many of Montana's contemporary tribes, including the Blackfeet, Assiniboine, Salish, Kootenai, Crow, and Shoshone, were in Montana by the Late Prehistoric period, if not before. Villages emerged on the Columbia Plateau of Idaho and Washington and in the Missouri River valley of North and South Dakota. Even though village archaeological sites are rare in Montana, hunter-gatherers from Montana participated in active trade with villagers from adjacent regions. Populations increased in Montana and Wyoming, resulting in heightened competition for resources and a higher proportion of archaeological skeletons with injuries from violent encounters.

The introduction and adoption of the horse between approximately 1650 and 1750 marks the end of the Late Prehistoric period. While European-Americans had been in the New World since 1492, their effects weren't felt in Montana until later. European diseases reached

Flathead camp in western Montana circa 1920s —Courtesy of Archives and Special Collections, Mansfield Library, University of Montana

Montana in the seventeenth century, and the horse at the beginning of the eighteenth. The introduction of the horse accompanied an influx of new Native American tribes to Montana, lured by ample bison and pushed westward by European-American encroachment.

History of Archaeological Research in Montana

Much is known about the early human history of Montana because of the work of numerous archaeologists, who have explored every nook and cranny of the West since the early twentieth century. Among the more important sites excavated anywhere in the United States during the first half of the twentieth century was the Folsom Site in Folsom, New Mexico. Here, in 1926, archaeologists from the Denver Museum of Natural History excavated bones of an extinct form of bison—*Bison antiquus*—along with fluted spear points called Folsom points. This was the first find that associated people with extinct fauna from approximately 11,000 to 10,000 years ago.

Before the Folsom Site discovery, many archaeologists believed that humans hadn't been in the Americas for more than a few thousand years. Archaeologists spent most of the early twentieth century looking for evidence of people from earlier times, but it wasn't until they found this extinct form of bison with a unique spear point at the Folsom Site that they successfully proved the antiquity of people in the Americas.

Archaeologists then realized that they had about 10,000 years of human history to explore, not only in New Mexico but in other states and the rest of the Americas as well.

During the Great Depression of the 1930s, President Franklin Roosevelt implemented the New Deal to put unemployed Americans back to work. The Works Progress Administration (WPA) funded infrastructure projects including highways, bridges, and buildings. The WPA also funded archaeological excavations, including two very important excavations in Montana: the Hagen and Pictograph Cave sites. Research at these sites helped fill gaps in our knowledge about the last 10,000 years in Montana.

Pictograph Cave is one of a series of cave openings in sandstone cliffs along the Yellowstone River near Billings. Oscar Lewis, a local rancher with a great interest in the archaeology of Montana, directed the excavation here between 1936 and 1941. During the early excavations, Lewis's team recovered nine human remains and more than thirty thousand artifacts. Among the artifacts was an amazing array of well-preserved organic materials, including cordage, bone, wood, and roots.

Excavations at Pictograph Cave in 1941 —Courtesy of Montana State Parks, a division of Montana Fish, Wildlife, and Parks

A small stone pendant with etched human face from Pictograph Cave
—Courtesy of Montana State Parks, a division of Montana Fish, Wildlife, and Parks

William Mulloy, who was hired to supervise the WPA-funded Montana Archaeological Survey projects in 1941, used the hundreds of projectile points found at Pictograph Cave to create the first cultural chronology of the region in 1958. This chronology included three periods: Early Prehistoric, Middle Prehistoric, and Late Prehistoric. Mulloy went on to become a professor of anthropology at the University of Wyoming in Laramie, teaching one of the most famous and important archaeologists of the current era, George C. Frison. Along with Carling Malouf and Frison, Mulloy can be considered a grandfather of Montana archaeology, even though most of his research was in Wyoming.

Between 1936 and 1938, Oscar Lewis was field director for the famous excavations at the Hagen Site near Glendive in far eastern Montana. The Hagen Site was one of the first excavations conducted by the Montana Archaeological Survey. As reported by William Mulloy in 1942, excavations at the Hagen Site revealed that it was probably affiliated with the Crow, and probably representative of their split in the fifteenth century from the Hidatsa, who then lived along the Missouri River. The Hagen Site was a village similar to others along the Missouri River, but it is also associated with large-scale bison hunting. Nearly thirty thousand pottery sherds (the archaeological term for shards) were collected at the Hagen Site.

Between approximately 1945 and 1970, archaeologists in Montana continued to excavate sites, collecting data in order to better understand where early peoples had lived in Montana and when they were here. William Mulloy continued to be a major force in Montana archaeology

William Mulloy
—Eric Carlson illustration

during this time. In addition, Carling Malouf emerged on the Montana archaeology scene, establishing the University of Montana (then Montana State University) Department of Anthropology. Malouf, along with archaeologists from the American Museum of Natural History and Columbia University, excavated the MacHaffie Site near Helena in the 1950s, collecting abundant archaeological material dating back to the Folsom Culture. Malouf pioneered the study of stone circles and rock art in western Montana, including the Flathead and Bitterroot valleys.

Richard Forbis, a student of Carling Malouf, participated in the excavations at the MacHaffie Site in the early 1950s. Forbis later taught two Montana archaeologists at the University of Calgary, Brian Reeves and Leslie Davis, both of whom have contributed greatly to our knowledge of the human history of Montana.

George C. Frison, one of the most important archaeologists of the last century, attended the University of Wyoming in the early 1960s and began teaching there in 1967. He conducted most of his archaeological work in Montana and Wyoming. Frison's 1991 book, *Prehistoric Hunters of the High Plains*, is a classic work based largely on his hundreds of excavations in the region.

Frison employs the New Archaeology theoretical perspective inspired by Lewis Binford in the 1960s and 1970s. New Archaeologists, also called Processual Archaeologists, approach their study by digging deeper into the meaning of archaeological discoveries. Rather than just answer questions of when and where, New Archaeology seeks to answer questions such as why and how. How and why did cultures change over time,

George C. Frison
—Eric Carlson illustration

and how can archaeological research contribute to a better understanding of subsistence, settlement, and technology?

Among George Frison's most famous excavations in Montana is the Mill Iron Site near Montana's border with the Dakotas. Frison and his team of archaeologists from the University of Wyoming recovered artifacts associated with the Goshen Culture, dating back 10,800 years or more. Frison's 1996 Mill Iron Site report is a classic of the New Archaeology, emphasizing an interdisciplinary approach to the study of not just stone and bone artifacts, but also pollen, plants, and the environment.

Since 1970, several other archaeologists have played important roles in the archaeology of Montana. Brian Reeves's work at the famous Head-Smashed-In Buffalo Jump in Alberta pioneered the study of buffalo jumps in the northwestern Great Plains. Alston Thoms and Randall Schalk completed archaeological studies in and around Lake Koocanusa near Libby. Leslie Davis from Montana State University in Bozeman has conducted numerous important excavations in the state, including work at the Schmitt chert quarry near Three Forks and at the Indian Creek Site south of Helena. Dee C. Taylor of the University of Montana conducted important projects along Lake Koocanusa in northwestern Montana and at Yellowstone National Park, while one of his students, Thomas Foor, pioneered the use of statistical methods and archaeological databases in Montana archaeology.

Sally Thompson Greiser has contributed greatly to the archaeology of Montana in her studies at the Sun River Site near Great Falls, while Stanley Ahler conducted important studies of pottery styles and Knife River Flint

SITE EXCAVATION

Archaeological excavation involves the careful removal of layers of dirt to uncover artifacts and features left by peoples of the past. These excavations must be conducted carefully so that artifacts from one layer are not accidentally mixed with artifacts from another layer. Very often, the same family or group used a site over and over again through time, and each use occurs in a layer. Archaeologists call each of those site uses an occupation. A number of occupations closely related in time and involving similar activities are collectively called a site component. Sometimes archaeological sites contain various site components in stratified levels, with older occupations found deeper and younger occupations more near the surface. Excavations of stratified sites can reach several feet deep. For example, Mummy Cave in Wyoming contained evidence of more than thirty occupations within roughly 27 feet of dirt. Archaeologists strive to understand what activities were conducted during each occupation and within each component of a site. By doing so, they can track change or continuity in cultures over time.

Features are an important part of understanding the past. A feature is the location of a specific activity. For example, a fire pit is a feature used in the past to provide heat or cook food. Fire pits often contain fire-cracked rock, charcoal, bones, and plant remains, which can tell archaeologists what kinds of activities were carried out at the site. Common features include storage pits, house pits, graves, and caches. When archaeologists find bones at sites, they try to determine the species of animal, its sex, its age, and other information that might provide insight into why the animal was hunted and killed. By recording the number and types of bones, archaeologists can also figure out the number of animals killed at a given location; this helps them understand how many people might have participated in the hunt and the community's needs in terms of meat. If one hundred bison were killed at a site, we can assume that many families were involved in the hunt. One hundred bison could feed dozens of people for many weeks.

Archaeological excavations are crucial to understanding prehistory, and they shouldn't be conducted without proper training. I recommend that everyone interested in archaeology participate in an archaeological field school, which will teach you how to conduct a proper excavation. Many universities throughout the country offer field schools. You should never dig at a site without proper training. If you find artifacts or an archaeological site, you should notify the landowner and the State Historic

11

Preservation Office. In Montana, the preservation office at the Montana Historical Society will provide you with forms so that you can record the site location and provide information about what you found. Every state in the country has a historic preservation office, and its job is to protect cultural resources, including archaeological sites. The staff will always be willing to help you protect and record an archaeological site.

The Archaeological Resource Protection Act was passed in 1979 to protect archaeological sites on federal land. The act makes it unlawful to take artifacts or conduct archaeological excavations without permits on federal and tribal lands. A permit can be earned only with proof of proper training. The National Historic Preservation Act was passed in 1966 to ensure that federal agencies take into account the effects of their projects on all cultural resources, including archaeological sites, traditional sites, and historic buildings. A federal agency cannot approve a project that would destroy an archaeological site without taking measures to protect or avoid the site. Many professional archaeologists working in Montana are employed by the federal government or are under contract to a federal agency to help find, protect, and excavate sites. Another important archaeology law is the Native American Graves Protection and Repatriation Act, passed in 1992 to protect Native American remains and associated artifacts.

use in eastern Montana and western North Dakota. Ann Johnson has edited the journal *Archaeology in Montana* for many years, making a major contribution to the published record.

Many archaeologists in Montana today work to help preserve cultural resources affected by projects involving federal permitting or oversight, such as highways, pipelines, and coal mines. Section 106 of the National Historic Preservation Act, passed by Congress in 1966, requires that federal agencies consider the effects of such projects on cultural resources, including archaeological sites. Compliance with this law typically entails archaeological surveys and excavations to ensure that archaeological sites are not destroyed in the project's construction. Much of my work at the University of Montana centers on teaching cultural resource management to students who will eventually work in that business. My project at Yellowstone National Park—the Montana-Yellowstone Archaeological Project—is designed to collect archaeological data from a cultural resource management perspective. Millions of dollars in funding are provided every year by federal agencies for archaeological survey and excavation projects.

The Montana Environment

Montana is composed of two parts: east and west. In the east, the Great Plains stretch from the Rocky Mountain Front to the eastern edge of the state and beyond. In the west, mountains abound. Most of Montana's archaeological sites have been found east of the Rocky Mountains, in the Great Plains. While people probably lived and traveled all across Montana during the last 11,000 years, sites are simply easier to find in the east because of the open terrain. The east may have seen more use as well, due to its great herds of bison. The mixed-grass prairie of the Great Plains has for thousands of years supported large herds of bison, the staple of early peoples' subsistence there. In the rugged Rocky Mountains of the western part of the state, archaeological sites are present but more difficult to find.

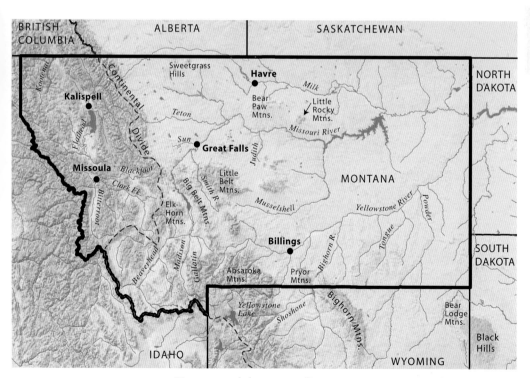

Montana and the surrounding area

The Yellowstone River near Gardiner

Water was also key to human survival in the Great Plains, and in eastern Montana all streams flow toward the Missouri, including such tributaries as the Milk, Sun, Bighorn, Powder, and Yellowstone rivers. Beginning in Three Forks—where the Gallatin, Jefferson, and Madison rivers have their confluence—the Missouri flows some 726 miles in Montana, continuing eastward through the Dakotas before joining the Mississippi River north of St. Louis, Missouri. West of the Continental Divide, water flows into the Columbia River Basin, which empties into the Pacific Ocean. The Bitterroot, Clark Fork, Blackfoot, Kootenai, and Flathead rivers in western Montana all are part of the Columbia River Basin. The state's many rivers and lakes provided a lifeline for people, and most important archaeological sites in Montana are found along waterways. Movement from place to place largely followed river corridors.

Eastward in the Dakotas, some early people chose to adopt agriculture and settled into villages over the last few thousand years. Meanwhile, native people in what is now Montana continued to hunt and gather their food. The climate contributed to the lack of agriculture. With low temperatures and low precipitation, Montana is not ideal for growing crops. Generally, prehistoric agriculture required more than 90 frost-free days and more than 20 inches of precipitation per year. Butte and Kalispell in the western part of the state get about 73 and 91 frost-free days per year, respectively, while Billings, in the east, gets 150. But in terms of precipitation, none of those three cities—Butte (13 inches), Kalispell (17 inches), and Billings (15 inches)—could support agriculture without irrigation.

It wasn't only the prohibitive climate, but also the wide availability of adequate sustenance provided by numerous wild plants and animals, that led Montana cultures to avoid agriculture. Why settle down and grow crops when prey species such as bison and edible plants such as bitterroot and camas were so plentiful?

In western Montana, hunter-gatherers collected the roots of camas and bitterroot in mass quantities in the spring when these blooming plants were easily found and harvested. Although lacking the western abundance of camas and bitterroot, eastern Montana has similar edible bulbs and roots, including wild onion, sego lily, and biscuitroot. Wild fruits including chokecherry, huckleberry, and prickly pear cactus also were important plant foods in Montana. Melvin Gilmore, a prominent ethnobotanist, has recorded more than 1,100 useful plants collected for use as food and medicine by early peoples of the northern Great Plains and Rocky Mountains.

Hunter-gatherers of Montana organized their movements according to when various plants were available for harvest, traveling through various environments on a seasonal cycle. While you might think of the hunter-gatherer lifestyle as one of unpredictability and uncertainty,

Camas in bloom at Lolo Pass on the Idaho-Montana border

Processed roots excavated from Pictograph Cave near Billings
—Courtesy of Montana State Parks, a division of Montana Fish, Wildlife, and Parks

people gathered sustenance on a generally regular schedule defined by knowledge of the environment. In the Bighorn Basin of Wyoming and Montana, people collected bitterroot, sego lily, onion, camas, and biscuitroot in the spring and early summer. From late summer to early fall, they gathered chokecherry, gooseberry, yucca seeds, and other plants and mixed them with meat to make pemmican. In late fall and early winter, wild rose hips, buffalo berries, and saltbush seeds were important plant foods.

Animal Hunting

While many different prey animals were available to hunter-gatherers in Montana, a small handful of species were the focus of hunting activities. West of the Continental Divide, deer, elk, trout, sheep, moose, and goat were the most commonly hunted species. East of the Continental Divide, the most dominant prey species included mule deer, whitetail deer, pronghorn, bighorn sheep, and, most important, bison. George Frison's research into the hunting of bison provides the basis for much of the following section.

Mule deer and whitetail deer were hunted during all seasons, in part because deer hide was preferred for clothing over the more widely available bison hide. Because deer spread out over a large territory and tend to hide during the day, favoring rough and brushy country, deer were stalked by individuals or small groups.

Pronghorn, colloquially known in the West as "antelope," were another dietary staple of Montana hunter-gatherers. Pronghorn favor open country, and herds of dozens of animals can be found on valley slopes in the Yellowstone valley north of Gardiner. Pronghorn are the fastest land animal in North America, with top speeds of more than 60 miles per hour, making them impossible to pursue on foot. Instead, hunters stalked pronghorn or lured them into traps. Pronghorn are extremely curious animals and can be easily convinced to investigate bright colors.

Pronghorn —National Park Service photo

Bighorn sheep, also called Rocky Mountain sheep, were an important prey species to prehistoric people, especially in the rugged uplands. Bighorn sheep tend to graze in open country on the edges of rugged country. If threatened, they will quickly retreat into uplands, where they are nimble climbers. Early hunters exploited the sheep's instinct to seek higher ground by using piles of converging rocks and brush, called drive lines, and corrals. Numerous high-altitude sheep hunting corrals and blinds are present in Montana and Wyoming. Some of these features show evidence of careful herding into corrals and subsequent dispatching using nets and clubs, in addition to projectile weaponry. Late fall, after the rut and before mountain snows, was the primary season for hunting sheep. Mummy Cave in northwestern Wyoming contains more than thirty stratigraphic layers showing abundant evidence of sheep hunting over the last 9,500 years.

While deer, pronghorn, and sheep were important prey species for many Montana hunter-gatherers, bison are generally considered the most important. Bison have been at the core of the Montana hunter-gatherer

Hunting blind used to hunt bighorn sheep near Dillon. Hunters hid in the pit and may have also added brush to the edges to help conceal them.

Bighorn sheep female (left) and male (right) in Yellowstone —National Park Service photo

diet for 11,000 years and were key to human survival in the Great Plains portion of Montana. Humans organized much of their travel and subsistence around the seasonal movements of bison. Their hunting strategies were so sophisticated that some view their control of bison as the beginnings of animal husbandry. While it is true that people were able to kill bison with the use of drive lines, jumps, and corrals, they did not control breeding of the animals, other than by rarely killing newborn calves in spring.

Bison were taken during all seasons but mostly from summer to early winter except during the rut, when male bison were unpredictable and mating hormones made the meat taste foul. Many kill sites were employed just after the rut, in late fall and early winter, when large herds of conjoined male and female bison provided prime targets for communal hunting strategies such as buffalo jumps. During winter, individuals and small groups hunted bison by stalking or surrounding the animals. Few hunts occurred in spring, the birthing season. Summer herds were hunted, especially in late summer, just before the rut.

The buffalo jump is the most common type of bison kill site in Montana, with hundreds of such sites in the state and the surrounding area. Most buffalo jumps share a similar structure, including a cliff, a large, flat upland above the cliff for setting drive lines, and a gathering basin adjacent to and including the drive lines. The gathering basins are

19

Bison in Yellowstone National Park

View to the west of Head-Smashed-In Buffalo Jump in Alberta

wide-open flat areas with ample grass and water to support large bison herds and help draw the bison in.

The hunters built rock drive lines that often led for miles from broad gathering basins to the edge of the cliff. Brush and occasionally fire would be employed along the drive lines to keep the bison from breaking out of the chutes; hunters would also stand along the drive lines to steer the bison toward the cliff.

Two types of jump were utilized: the jump and the pound. Some jumps—such as Head-Smashed-In—were tall cliffs over which bison were run in herds to their deaths. Other jumps included corrals, called pounds, which bison were herded into after being driven over a steep hillside or into a steep stream drainage or arroyo. Pounds were often built of wood and typically measured 3 to 5 feet in height—just tall enough to prevent

A gathering basin and rock drive line leading over Keough Buffalo Jump near Nye, Montana

bison from escaping. Once the animals were run over the cliff or into the arroyo, they found themselves in the pound, where they were killed by waiting hunters. Numerous pound sites have been identified in Montana and Wyoming, including the Wahkpa Chu'gn Buffalo Jump near Havre, Montana.

Native American use of the whole bison, with little or nothing going to waste, is renowned. While such efficiency might be exaggerated—some sites show a preference in which parts of bison were utilized—hunter-gatherers had uses for all parts of bison. Bison hides were used for clothing and for covering structures. Sinew was used to make tools and clothing. Meat was used for many varieties of food, including pemmican, which could be stored and saved for times of need, such as harsh winters. Pemmican was prepared by separating the fat and meat of the bison, drying the meat by hanging and smoking, and rendering the fat by boiling. After preparing the meat and fat, the products were mixed back together, with berries such as chokecherries added for flavor. The final mixture was then dried in portable portions and stored for use in winter and during travel, when food might be scarce. Evidence of pemmican preparation has been found at numerous archaeological sites in Montana, including the Wahkpa Chu'gn Buffalo Jump.

While bison provided clothing, tools, and food, the animal's spiritual importance to the people who relied on them cannot be overestimated. Bison are at the center of spiritual life for many Native American tribes in Montana.

Stone and Stone Tools

One of the most important aspects of human survival in Montana was the manufacture of stone tools such as projectile points, knives, and hide scrapers. The study of stone tools and how they were used helps archaeologists better understand human activities, including subsistence, settlement, travel, and trade patterns. Archaeologists study not only the finished tools but also the by-products of tool manufacture, known as debitage, or flaking debris. Debitage provides information about how the stone tools were made and often is the most abundant artifact found at archaeological sites. For example, production of a single projectile point generated hundreds of pieces of flaking debris, many of which may be later found by archaeologists.

During human prehistory in Montana, projectile points typically were used with three types of implements: atlatl darts, spears, and arrows. The atlatl, a handle that allowed hunters to throw their killing darts farther and more accurately than they could throw a spear, was used with great success for thousands of years in Montana. If you've ever seen anyone throwing a ball to a dog using a throwing stick, you've seen the atlatl principle in action. The dart was secured in a notch at the end of a wooden throwing board with a handle. The spear point was hafted to the dart tip. The spear is similar to the atlatl but did not involve the use of a handle and throwing board. It was less accurate than the atlatl and generally used for close-encounter hunting or the final killing of injured animals. Bow and arrow technology developed in the Arctic and southwestern United States prior to its adoption in Montana approximately 1,500 years ago. Most hunters quickly adopted the bow and arrow because it provided numerous advantages over the atlatl, including increased accuracy and the ability to hide while hunting. The atlatl required that the hunter be standing and exposed to prey, whereas the bow and arrow provided increased efficiency and secrecy. The atlatl largely disappeared after adoption of the bow and arrow.

The atlatl
—Eric Carlson illustration

The bow and arrow
—Eric Carlson illustration

Each of these hunting implements—the atlatl, spear, and bow and arrow—required killing tips or projectile points produced from stone. As such, stone acquisition was an important aspect of daily life. Amazingly, the early toolmakers knew the locations of all the major sources of stone with the qualities necessary for tools.

Materials used for stone tool manufacture in Montana and nearby states include volcanic rocks such as obsidian, basalt, andesite, dacite,

---

THE MANUFACTURE OF STONE TOOLS

The manufacture of stone tools involved several steps, the first of which was obtaining stone at quarries. Prior to making tools, hunter-gatherers improved the quality of some stones by heating them at very high temperatures. Heat treatment made the stone easier to work. While unnecessary for obsidian, which is pure glass, heat treatment was sometimes used to remove impurities in cherts. At quarry locations, hunter-gatherers would often shape the stone into the rough form, or preform, of a tool. By producing preforms at quarries, they reduced the amount of stone they had to carry with them when they left the quarry.

Two common tool types found at archaeological sites in Montana are the biface and uniface. Bifaces—tools flaked on two sides—could be used as knives, projectile points, and preform for other tools. Unifaces—flaked on one side—were used as cutting, scraping, or butchering tools. Early toolmakers called flintknappers produced unifaces and bifaces by removing flakes from the stone. To do this, they struck the rock at the proper angle and with proper force with a hammer, such as a stream cobble or the butt end of an elk antler. After using tools for a while, hunter-gatherers often retouched or sharpened them by removing small flakes from the tool edge. By studying the flakes found at archaeological sites, we can understand the technology early humans used to produce their tools.

Archaeologists often conduct experiments in stone tool manufacture and use to better understand the process. When I was in graduate school, I used stone tools to butcher animals so I could understand the wear patterns generated on the tools. Using my experimental tools as a guide, I was able to analyze prehistoric stone tool wear patterns to determine what the tools had been used for. Another way to understand stone tool function is to analyze blood proteins found on them. Through such analysis, archaeologists can identify what species were hunted or butchered using the tool.

and rhyolite; a variety of cherts, such as chalcedony, composed of cryptocrystalline silica, and petrified wood, a chert that forms when silica
replaces the cellular structure of wood; and quartzite, a metamorphosed
sandstone. Obsidian, basalt, chert, and quartzite were the most common
materials used for stone tool manufacture in Montana.

One of the most interesting aspects of the study of stone tools is the
identification of the specific type of rock used and its place of origin in
order to trace human movements. By understanding where the rock used
to make tools came from, we can decipher where their makers traveled
and traded and what their territories were. The study of stone and its use
by early peoples is an important focus of many archaeologists in Montana.

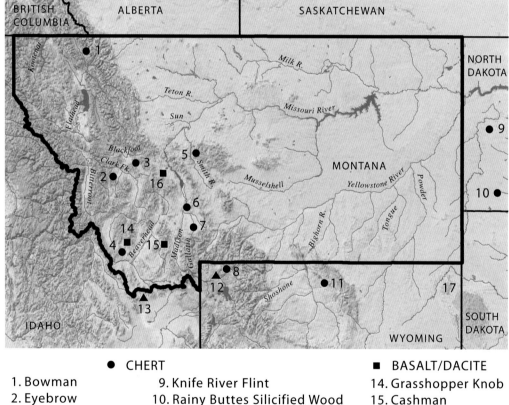

● CHERT		■ BASALT/DACITE
1. Bowman	9. Knife River Flint	14. Grasshopper Knob
2. Eyebrow	10. Rainy Buttes Silicified Wood	15. Cashman
3. Avon	11. Big Horn Phosphoria	16. Grady Ranch
4. South Everson		
5. Smith River Quarries		ORTHOQUARTZITE
6. Schmitt; Logan	▲ OBSIDIAN	17. Bear Lodge Mtns.
7. Lime Creek	12. Obsidian Cliff	
8. Crescent Hill	13. Bear Gulch	

Major stone sources in Montana and the surrounding region

*Obsidian from Obsidian Cliff in Wyoming, one of the
most important sources of stone in the region*

To identify a source outcrop of obsidian, trace elements within the artifact are compared with those in known sources of obsidian. In Yellowstone National Park, for example, lots of artifacts were produced from obsidian from Obsidian Cliff (also in the park), one of the most prolific and important stone sources in the region. However, some artifacts found in the park are made of obsidian from Bear Gulch in Idaho or from Big Southern Butte near Idaho Falls, more than 300 miles south of Yellowstone.

In addition to the widely used obsidian, several other stones were important in this region. Knife River Flint from western North Dakota—a brown, translucent chalcedony that forms from the silicification of peat—is widespread at archaeological sites in eastern Montana and is found at sites hundreds of miles from its source area. Other source-specific stones utilized in eastern Montana and western North Dakota include Swan River chert, Tongue River silicified sediment, and Rainy Buttes silicified wood. Gray and red porcellanite, which is clay that has been baked by a burned coal seam, is common in eastern Montana, while quartzite is available at a variety of outcrops in Wyoming and Montana.

Sources for the volcanic rocks basalt, andesite, and dacite are also common in southwestern Montana near Dillon, Ennis, and Bozeman. A few dacite outcrops have been studied via X-ray fluorescence analysis, revealing unique trace-element compositions that can be used to identify the source of stone artifacts. The Cashman Quarry in Madison County and the Grady Ranch Quarry near Helena are the best-documented of these dacite quarries.

Knife River Flint, a type of chalcedony from western North Dakota

Middle Archaic projectile point of the McKean Culture, produced from dacite from the Cashman Quarry. The point was recovered in the Yellowstone valley north of Gardiner.

A variety of crypocrystalline silica materials—or cherts—occur in Montana. Many are labeled Montana cherts and are indistinguishable from each other. Several of the Montana cherts occur within the prominent Madison Limestone, a formation located along the Rocky Mountain Front between Glacier and Yellowstone national parks. Hunter-gatherers, the original hard-rock miners of the Big Sky State, utilized these chert quarries, often large pits, extensively. These pits suggest intensive exploitation of the rock for trade and tool manufacture. Tom Roll and his colleagues at Montana State University have studied six important chert quarries in Montana: the Eyebrow, Avon, and South Everson Creek quarries in western Montana, and the Smith River, Logan, and Lime Creek quarries in central Montana. In general cherts are not as amenable to source identification as volcanic materials, but Roll has successfully identified trace element profiles of the South Everson Creek, Avon, and Lime Creek quarries.

In 2006, Yellowstone National Park archaeologists Ann Johnson, Robin Park, and Elaine Hale identified the Crescent Hill chert outcrop in the northern portion of the park, approximately 20 miles east of Mammoth Hot Springs. In 2009, the University of Montana mapped the encompassing Crescent Hill basalt formation, identifying nine surface chert outcrops, five of which showed evidence of quarrying. In consort

Pit excavated at the South Everson Creek chert quarry near Dillon

Crescent Hill chert outcrop in Yellowstone National Park

with Richard Hughes, an X-ray fluorescence analyst in California, the University of Montana evaluated whether the Crescent Hill chert has any unique trace elements that could help identify projectiles made from it. Because this chert formed within a basalt formation, it was thought to hold trace elements of the parent volcanic material. If so, it would have become one of only a handful of cherts in the United States whose source could be successfully identified via the X-ray fluorescence method. Preliminary results of this study show that Crescent Hill chert lacks the trace elements that help pinpoint sources. For now, it looks like Crescent Hill chert is just another Montana chert.

What is clear from the archaeological data is that the early inhabitants of Montana knew where to find high-quality stone. Archaeologists have found numerous projectile points made of stone with yet-unidentified geologic sources, suggesting that there are more quarry sites to be located.

Rock Art

Another important aspect of early life in Montana is the production of art, including textiles, painted robes, portable objects, and images on rock. The archaeological record in Montana is especially prolific with sites containing rock art—pictographs (painted images on rock faces) and petroglyphs (images incised on rock faces). Rock art was typically produced in places considered special or striking landscapes, reflecting the often-spiritual nature of the art. The art may have represented a historical narrative of important events, or it may have been made by religious leaders or vision-seeking individuals. James Keyser, Julie Francis, Mavis and John Greer, and Larry Loendorf are a few of the more prominent rock art researchers in the Montana region and have published excellent books and research on the topic.

Determining the age of rock art is extremely difficult, especially if it is very old, produced during the Paleoindian and Archaic periods. A huge variety of environmental factors—wind, heat, lichens, bugs, graffiti—can affect rock art over time. In general, the more recently the rock art was made, the better the chance it will have been preserved. Radiocarbon dating can be used to date only paints made with organic material, but most pictographs were painted with inorganic material such as ochre. Rock art is more commonly dated through association with sites of known age. Also, certain styles of art are associated with certain cultures. If one style is superimposed over another style, archaeologists know its relative age.

A relatively new means of dating rock art, called cation-ratio dating, has been used at some of the more important rock art sites in the northern Great Plains. Cation-ratio dating measures the leaching of potassium and calcium out of rock varnish and compares the ratios of those elements to that of titanium, which does not leach. Dates acquired with the cation-ratio method are often disregarded because the vagaries of

Kila Pictographs near Kalispell, Montana

local environment can influence varnish formation rates. To arrive at an accurate date, scientists must analyze the local rates of varnish formation. They did this in the Bighorn Basin of northwestern Wyoming and south-central Montana, which has some of the earliest rock art in North America. None of this art has been dated to the Paleoindian period, but two examples are more than 6,000 years old. Rock art dating to the last 2,000 years is much more common in Montana.

The Earliest Peoples of Montana

The Paleoindian Period

11,000 TO 8,000 YEARS AGO

The record of Paleoindians in Montana is growing larger every year, with the existing data suggesting a diverse subsistence pattern between approximately 11,000 and 8,000 years ago. Some Paleoindian sites are classic bison kill sites of the Great Plains, while others in the uplands show evidence of a variety of animal and plant foods. The oldest known site in the state, dated to 11,040 years ago, is a burial cache suggesting ceremonial behavior. We know people lived here and we know a little bit about how they lived, but who were Montana's earliest peoples and where did they come from?

Until about 1995, most archaeologists believed that people of the Clovis Culture were the first to settle the Americas. While Clovis seems to have been the first culture in Montana, around 11,000 years ago, several archaeological sites have shown that people were in other parts of the Americas before hunter-gatherers of the Clovis Culture arrived. The earliest archaeological site in North America, Paisley Caves in Oregon, dates to more than 12,000 years old. A site in South America, Monte Verde near the Pacific Ocean in Chile, also dates to 12,000 years ago. While there are a few other accepted pre-Clovis sites in the Americas, these two are the best of the best.

Archaeologists from the University of Oregon investigated Paisley Caves, in the northern part of the Great Basin, in the early 2000s. They collected desiccated feces from the cave that were 12,300 years old. Analysis of the feces revealed human mitochondrial DNA, proving that humans were at the site. This is the oldest incontrovertible evidence of human occupation of North America. The mitochondrial DNA showed that the earliest occupants of the western United States came from Asia, most likely traveling the Pacific Coast from northeastern Asia—perhaps from Siberia, Kamchatka Peninsula, or Hokkaido (Japan's northernmost island).

The Monte Verde Site in Chile supports the theory of migration along the Pacific Coast. Monte Verde is located on a terrace of Chinchihuapi Creek approximately 30 miles inland from the Pacific Ocean. Tom Dillehay of the University of Kentucky excavated the site in the 1980s and

1990s, yielding numerous artifacts dating to approximately 12,500 years ago. Among the artifacts were stone tools, textiles, human footprints, edible plants, faunal remains, and post molds of shelters. David Meltzer of Southern Methodist University and several colleagues visited the site to corroborate Dillehay's findings. Their confirmation of the antiquity and legitimacy of Monte Verde made it the earliest accepted archaeological site in the Americas, and the first to counter the theory that the Clovis were first.

Early Paleoindian Period

Clovis Culture

While Monte Verde and Paisley Caves indicate human occupation of the Pacific Coast before 12,000 years ago, the earliest archaeological sites in Montana date to the Clovis period, between approximately 11,200 and 10,900 years ago. In fact the earliest sites in all of the Rocky Mountains and the Great Plains—from Alberta to Texas and from Missouri to Idaho—date to the Clovis period. While people apparently arrived at the west coast of the Americas prior to 12,000 years ago, it may have taken them several hundred years to make their way inland. Clovis sites are often identified by distinctive large projectile points that are lanceolate, meaning they are long and taper to a tip, like a lance.

The origin of Montana's first peoples is controversial. The earliest Clovis sites in the United States—all dating to about 11,300 to 11,100 years ago—are in Florida, Montana, and South Dakota. Other Clovis-age sites all across the country date to just after this time, suggesting nearly instantaneous population of North America by the Clovis. Because of this, it has been difficult to determine the direction from which the Clovis arrived in Montana. Two likely scenarios are migration from the north via an ice-free corridor from Alaska, or migration from the Pacific coast up major river valleys such as the Columbia. A third, less likely scenario is that the Clovis originated in the east from an Upper Paleolithic European ancestral population dubbed the Solutrean. This theory is not well supported by the archaeological data but continues to be investigated by researchers such as the Smithsonian Institution's Dennis Stanford and well-known archaeologist Bruce Bradley.

While there are some similarities in the stone and bone tool technology of the European Solutrean and the American Clovis, they are probably the result of independent invention rather than cultural association. Recent investigations of stone artifact styles in Alaska, including the Denali and Nenana complexes, have shown similarities with Clovis, suggesting a north-to-south migration. Such sites as Broken Mammoth in Alaska support such a scenario, yielding radiocarbon dates of approximately 11,700 years ago.

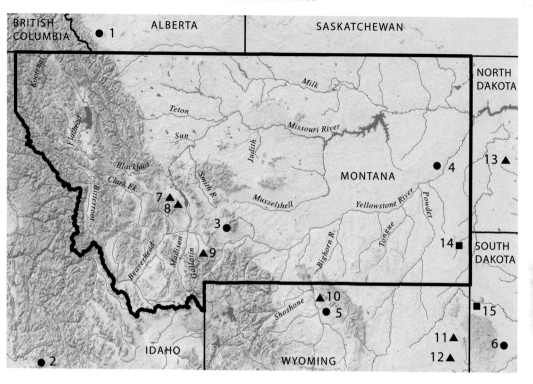

- ● CLOVIS
  1. Wally's Beach
  2. Simon
  3. Anzick
  4. Lindsay Mammoth
  5. Colby
  6. Lange-Ferguson

- ▲ FOLSOM
  7. MacHaffie
  8. Indian Creek
  9. King
  10. Hanson
  11. Agate Basin
  12. Hell Gap
  13. Big Black/Bobtail Wolf

- ■ GOSHEN
  14. Mill Iron
  15. Jim Pitts

Clovis, Goshen, and Folsom sites in Montana and the surrounding region

To get from interior Alaska to the Great Plains, people would have traveled through an inhospitable ice-free corridor that existed between the Laurentide and Cordilleran glaciers. Carole Mandryk has shown that the corridor would have supported human populations after about 11,500 years ago. Traveling through the corridor would have brought people directly to southern Alberta and Montana, where two of the earliest Clovis sites in North America have been found: the Anzick Site north of Livingston near Wilsall, Montana, and the Wally's Beach Site in southern Alberta near the Montana border.

An alternative scenario involving the migration of peoples up the Columbia River Basin through the Rocky Mountains to Montana is possible but not well supported. Clovis sites are uncommon west of the Rockies.

Migration through the interior Canadian corridor was slow—a few miles per year on average. People may have remained in the same general area for generations before exploring farther south and liking what they saw. To the people who made this journey, this trip was in all likelihood nothing more than the occupation of the same space. They lived and died within a landscape familiar to them. Montana's first inhabitants moved slowly, almost imperceptibly southward from northeastern Asia between 12,000 and 11,000 years ago.

While not plentiful, cache sites and kill sites associated with mammoth remains provide a decent picture of Clovis life in the Great Plains and Rockies during the initial period of human occupation. Clovis people left behind caches of stone and bone tools used for either funtional or ceremonial or other ritualistic reasons. They also hunted a variety of now-extinct ice-age animals, including mammoth, horse, and camel.

Some researchers, foremost among them Paul S. Martin of the University of Arizona, have suggested that it is more than coincidence that the arrival of people in North America occurred nearly simultaneously with the extinction of thirty-five species of megafauna approximately 11,000 years ago, including saber-toothed cats, dire wolves, and mammoths. However, while Martin's overkill hypothesis may explain the demise of the mammoth, there is little to no evidence that people contributed to the demise of other megafauna in the Americas. For example, giant sloths went extinct as well, but the remains of these animals are extremely rare in archaeological assemblages. If humans drove them into

Mammoth —Eric Carlson illustration

extinction, where are the kill sites as evidence? Recent data from several Clovis-period sites throughout the Americas suggest that an asteroid may have played a substantial role in the extinctions.

Richard Firestone of the University of California, in consort with colleagues including C. Vance Haynes of the University of Arizona, has evaluated the hypothesis that an asteroid explosion above the ice sheet in southern Canada may have caused substantial environmental changes approximately 10,800 years ago. Haynes reports a dark soil horizon, which he calls the "black mat," at more than fifty excavated sites in the Americas, including the MacHaffie, Sun River, Indian Creek, and Lindsay Mammoth sites in Montana. The black mat signifies a cooler climate with decreased evaporation of groundwater and an associated increase in plant biomass. Across the world, the period between 10,800 and 10,200 years ago is linked to a cool, dry period called the Younger Dryas. Only recently have scientists linked the start of the Younger Dryas to a possible asteroid impact. Evidence compiled by Firestone and colleagues includes magnetic soil grains with iridium, magnetic microspherules, and nanodiamonds, all of which are extraterrestrial in origin.

The cause of the megafauna extinctions of 10,800 years ago remains uncertain and is a major point of debate in American archaeology, but the events of the time clearly impacted people. Archaeologists have not found Clovis points, Clovis caches, or mammoth kills younger than 10,800 years.

ANZICK SITE

The Anzick Site near Wilsall is the oldest well-dated archaeological site in Montana, yielding radiocarbon dates of 11,040 years ago. The Anzick Site is the only Clovis site excavated in Montana. The Lindsay Mammoth Site, near Lindsay in eastern Montana, dates to about 11,200 years ago but lacks clear association with people and is likely a purely paleontological find, not an archaeological one. Not only is the Anzick Site the earliest known Clovis site in Montana, it has also yielded the oldest human remains found anywhere in North America. Excavators at the site, including Robson Bonnichsen of Oregon State University and Larry Lahren of Livingston, discovered the remains of a two-year-old infant buried with more than one hundred artifacts, including Clovis fluted projectile points, bone and antler tools, and large stone knives, in a ritual cache. Lahren and Bonnichsen suggest that antler rods from the site are foreshafts of atlatl darts. The artifacts, typical of other Clovis cache sites in western North America, are among the most finely crafted items from the early history of Montana. Some are decorated with red ochre. It seems fairly clear that they were placed with the infant as part of a ritual or ceremony.

Clovis point from the cache at the Anzick Site —Courtesy of Juliet Morrow

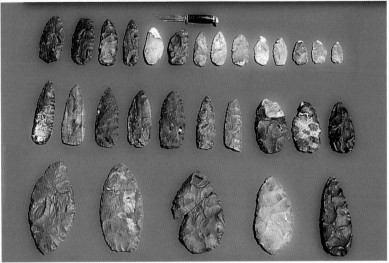

Bifaces (knives) recovered from the Clovis cache at the Anzick Site. Note knife at top for scale. —Photo © 2006 by Larry Lahren

Similar Clovis cache sites have been found in central Washington at the Richey-Roberts Site, in Wyoming at the Fenn Site, in Idaho at the Simon Site, and in Colorado at the Mahaffy Site. Human remains have been found only in the Anzick cache. Based on the discovery of human remains in the Clovis cache at the Anzick Site, some researchers have suggested that these Clovis sites are probably all burials. The caches have also been interpreted as stores of supplies or trail or place markers for Clovis people.

WALLY'S BEACH AND OTHER CLOVIS KILL SITES

Among the more interesting Clovis sites is the controversial Wally's Beach Site in Alberta, approximately 30 miles north of the Montana state line. This site has yielded bones of extinct ice-age animals radiocarbon dated at between 11,350 and 10,980 years old, making it among the oldest Clovis sites anywhere in North America. The bones and footprints of extinct animals, including horse and mammoth, were found with Clovis projectile points that contained the residue of blood protein from horse and bison. Some archaeologists question the association of the Clovis points with the animal remains because the points were found on or near the ground surface rather than excavated from layers with good stratigraphic integrity. Nevertheless, Clovis points with animal protein were found near extinct horse remains.

Wally's Beach is representative of other mammoth kill sites in the region, including the Colby Site, excavated by George Frison in the Bighorn Basin of northern Wyoming. The Colby Site contained the remains of seven mammoths with a mean radiocarbon age of 10,831 years, as well as camel and horse remains. The Clovis hunters apparently organized the mammoths into piles or meat caches for later use but never returned to collect their stores. The Lange-Ferguson Site in South Dakota includes the remains of two mammoths with a mean radiocarbon age of 11,100 years, while the Union Pacific Site in southern Wyoming yielded two mammoths with a radiocarbon age of 11,280 years. Finally, the Sheaman Site in east-central Wyoming contained a small Clovis camp recently dated to 11,200 years ago.

Goshen Culture

Hunter-gatherers appear to have adapted to the dramatic climate change of the Younger Dryas 10,800 years ago by beginning to hunt the one megafauna species that survived the mass extinction: *Bison antiquus*. Projectile points found in association with the bison remains are similar to Clovis points but lack the distinctive Clovis fluting and flaking technology. These large lanceolate points, called Goshen projectile points after Goshen County, Wyoming, exhibit parallel flaking. Archaeologists think the Goshen people were cultural descendants of Clovis. At Mill Iron, a Goshen site in eastern Montana, a mammoth rib fragment was found, indicating that individuals at the site carried a memento passed down from the period of Clovis mammoth hunting. Perhaps an elder at Mill Iron had even hunted mammoths prior to their extinction.

Goshen projectile point from the Mill Iron Site —Courtesy of Bureau of Land Management, Billings and Miles City offices

MILL IRON SITE

The second-oldest archaeological site in Montana—behind Anzick—is the Goshen-age Mill Iron Site in southeastern Montana near where the state line intersects with the South Dakota–North Dakota border. The Mill Iron Site, excavated by veteran researcher George Frison and his colleagues from the University of Wyoming, is one of the most valuable excavations ever to occur in the state. Radiocarbon dates on bison bones at the site range from approximately 11,300 to 10,800 years ago; however, the presence of a coal seam near the site has led most researchers, including Frison, to discard the oldest dates because of possible contamination by the coal, which is old carbon, after all. The widely accepted date for Mill Iron is approximately 10,840 years ago. The massive bison bone bed contains at least thirty bison, all adults and mostly cows, from a spring to early summer kill event. Low-value animal parts dominate at the kill site, suggesting that the hunters took the best parts of the animals with them when they left.

The assemblage of stone tools at Mill Iron comprised 1,709 pieces, including 31 Goshen projectile points, 5 bifaces, and 36 tools used in the butchering of bison. Most of the raw stone at the site was obtained locally. In contrast, Clovis sites typically contain very high-quality stone obtained from distant sources.

Environmental studies at the Mill Iron Site yielded significant data regarding the types of plants present in eastern Montana at the end of the ice age. The black mat soil associated with the Younger Dryas was not found at Mill Iron, and pollen and plant remains indicate a fairly warm climate and a landscape dominated by sagebrush. There is little data from the site to support the presence of the Younger Dryas in eastern Montana approximately 10,840 years ago. However, the evidence may indicate the anomalous climate of a single year or a specific region.

OTHER GOSHEN SITES

Several other Goshen-age archaeological sites have been excavated in the northwestern Great Plains, including Hell Gap and Carter/Kerr-McGee in Wyoming, Jim Pitts in South Dakota, and Upper Twin Mountain in Colorado. All of these sites have yielded Goshen projectile points in association with bison kills dating to between 10,800 and 10,400 years ago. The Upper Twin Mountain Site, excavated by Marcel Kornfeld and the University of Wyoming, yielded fifteen adult *Bison antiquus* killed between late fall and early winter approximately 10,400 years ago. This site is very similar to Mill Iron and probably marks the southern extent of Goshen sites in the Great Plains.

Folsom Culture

The Folsom period in Montana dates from approximately 10,900 to 10,200 years ago. In addition to Montana, Folsom people occupied more than 400,000 square miles from northern Texas to southern Manitoba and from Wisconsin to Idaho and New Mexico. Across this region, Folsom sites predominantly contain the remains of bison and occasionally other game. Since 1926, Folsom Culture has been a popular topic of study among North American archaeologists. Not only does Folsom represent one of the earliest well-established Paleoindian cultures of the Americas, but Folsom hunter-gatherers were specialized big-game hunters who utilized a remarkable projectile point.

Folsom hunter-gatherers produced one of the most distinctive projectile points in world history: the fluted Folsom point. Both Clovis and Folsom points have extremely fine pressure flaking, finely thinned bases, and channel flakes, but Folsom flintknappers took Clovis thinning and fluting to an extremely sophisticated level, removing a channel flake that progressed from the concave base to nearly the tip of the point. While

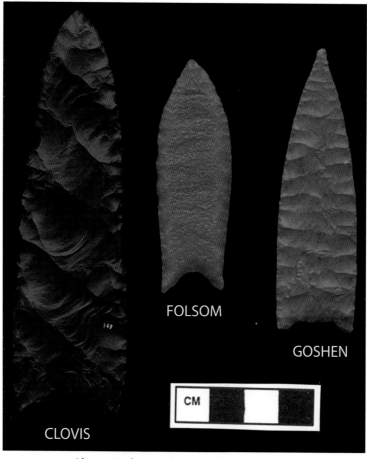

Clovis, Goshen, and Folsom projectile points

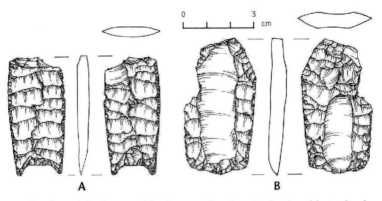

Sketches of the front and back, as well as longitudinal and latitudinal profiles, of two points: an unfluted Folsom point (A) and a fluted Folsom point preform (B) from the King Site —Courtesy of Matthew J. Root and Leslie B. Davis; Sarah Moore illustration

most Folsom projectile points were fluted, most Folsom sites also yield unfluted varieties of Folsom points. The technological similarities of Clovis and Folsom, as well as the chronological sequence of the two cultural complexes, support the hypothesis that Folsom fluting is a cultural descendant of Clovis flaked-stone technology.

Why did the Folsom people flute their points? Several archaeologists have successfully demonstrated the prowess of the fluted Folsom point. For example, Stanley Ahler and Phil Geib's replicative studies reveal that Folsom technology was well suited to the demands of bison hunting. While the fluted Folsom point was functionally successful, a variety of other projectile points without flutes were also used with great success for thousands of years by Great Plains bison hunters. Thus, despite Ahler and Geib's proposition of Folsom point superiority, it seems unlikely that the fluted Folsom point was any more efficient at killing prey than Clovis or Goshen points, or the succeeding Agate Basin, Hell Gap, or Scottsbluff points. Each of these point styles was used by Paleoindians for hunting similar prey, and each persisted as the preferred point form for several hundred years. In fact, archaeological sites yield greater numbers of bison before Folsom and after Folsom than during the Folsom period.

Because fluting does not appear to have provided an advantage to hunters and thus does not seem to have been a strictly technological adaptation, archaeologists have spent a great deal of time attempting to figure out why Folsom points were fluted at all. Much of this energy has been devoted to replicative studies of Folsom point manufacture. These experiments indicate that Folsom point production was extremely wasteful and risky, with breakage rates of 30 to 60 percent. Most production mishaps occurred during fluting, after significant energy had already been expended during the manufacture of the point preform. As Douglas Bamforth and Peter Bleed suggested in 1997, "There appears to be no reason to suppose that the increased procurement and production costs associated with fluted points were compensated by practical benefits."

The presence of discrete fluting production areas at several Folsom sites indicates that fluting may have been a special activity. Archaeologists can identify where the points were fluted by the presence of channel flakes—distinctive flakes removed from Folsom points during the fluting process. Finding a channel flake at a site is equivalent to finding a Folsom point; archaeologists know that the channel flake was created during the manufacture of a Folsom projectile point. Near Dunn Center, North Dakota, approximately 30 miles east of the Montana state line, teams from Washington State University, Northern Arizona University, and the University of North Dakota uncovered a series of substantial Folsom occupations in the Knife River Flint Quarries. Of particular importance, the Big Black and Bobtail Wolf sites yielded abundant evidence of Folsom tool manufacturing associated with the nearby quarries. At Bobtail Wolf, individuals crafted the early and middle stages of the points, called Folsom preforms, with comparatively little fluting. Individuals at the nearby Big Black Site focused their energies on fluting, and there is comparatively little evidence of early and middle stage preform manufacture. The process of fluting seems to have been spatially segregated between the two sites. Some individuals at Big Black fluted their projectile points from both the distal (haft) and proximal ends of both faces; such double fluting at Big Black may indicate that it was done as instruction or as a means to impress peers.

This spatial organization of knapping activities at Bobtail Wolf and Big Black resembles that of the Folsom component at the Agate Basin Site in Wyoming, where channel flakes were clustered in two discrete production areas, including one area that was separated from daily activities. At the Barger Gulch Site in Colorado, channel flakes were apparently deposited in special-use areas. At these Great Plains Folsom sites, fluting was squarely in the realm of specialized or segregated activities, perhaps associated with teaching or other sociocultural processes of the Folsom people. I hope that examination of this small sample of Folsom sites will inspire closer study of other Folsom assemblages to better understand the precise role of fluting within Folsom society, especially whether it was a task delegated to specialists or one open to any stone tool producer.

INDIAN CREEK SITE

The Indian Creek Site south of Helena yielded a radiocarbon date of approximately 10,805 years, making it one of the oldest Folsom sites anywhere in the Great Plains. Excavated in the 1980s by Leslie Davis and colleagues from Montana State University in Bozeman, the site is located in the valley of Indian Creek, a tributary of the Missouri River,

Indian Creek Site

within the foothills of the Elkhorn Mountains. Studies of pollen from the site suggest it was pine forest, much as it is today. Along with the nearby MacHaffie Site, Indian Creek provides a glimpse of Folsom adaptation to higher elevations in the northwestern Great Plains and Rocky Mountain regions. While bison was definitely the food of choice for Folsom hunters on the open plains, the food base diversified greatly in the mountains and foothills to include marmot, jackrabbit, and bighorn sheep. The Folsom occupations occur near the bottom of the soil profile, above a stratigraphic layer of ash dated to around 11,125 years ago and sourced to Glacier Peak, a volcano in the Cascade Range. The site shows incredible stratigraphic depth and provides an example of outstanding archaeological excavation by a team from Montana.

The site yielded three broken Folsom points and seven channel flakes. In addition to the point manufacture debris, Indian Creek yielded four bifaces and a small assortment of endscrapers, sidescrapers, knives, and gravers, indicating a wide array of tool activities. Chert from the local Madison Formation accounted for nearly 70 percent of the stone tool assemblage, with few identifiable nonlocal materials. This lack of exotics suggests that the camp's inhabitants moved mostly within the vicinity of the Indian Creek Site. The presence of a wide variety of prey additionally suggests a well-adapted subsistence pattern and long-term use of the area or similar environments. The site also yielded evidence of later occupations dated between 7,000 and 6,400 years ago, though these occupations aren't well documented.

MACHAFFIE SITE

Also located in the Elkhorn Mountains south of Helena, the MacHaffie Site was excavated primarily in the 1950s, with brief revisits in the 1960s and 1970s. Carling Malouf of the University of Montana was among the first to conduct excavations there, together with his colleague Richard Forbis. Forbis and John Sperry report the presence of twenty-five artifacts that can be solidly linked to the Folsom occupation, which directly underlies a later Cody Complex occupation. Among these twenty-five artifacts are a partial Folsom point preform, two Folsom bases, and a channel flake. Three of the artifacts were produced from "dark green flint with exceptionally fine crystalline structure." The point preform and the channel flake were recovered during excavations; an additional fluted Folsom point was recovered by the landowner in a creek bed near the site. A small number of endscrapers and sidescrapers were also found, suggesting that Folsom individuals prepared hides at the site.

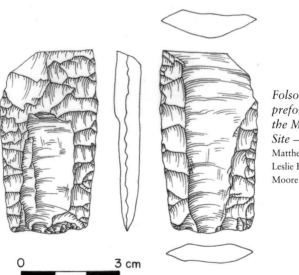

Folsom point preform from the MacHaffie Site —Courtesy of Matthew J. Root and Leslie B. Davis; Sarah Moore illustration

0   3 cm

In the 1990s, Leslie Davis conducted additional work at the MacHaffie Site. Two radiocarbon dates from bison bone were assayed by Davis, yielding dates of 10,390 and 10,090 years ago, making it one of the more recent Folsom sites in the region. Excavators at the site report the recovery of bison, deer, rabbit, and wolf bones from the Folsom levels, as a well as a riparian pollen suite suggestive of a wet upland streamside setting.

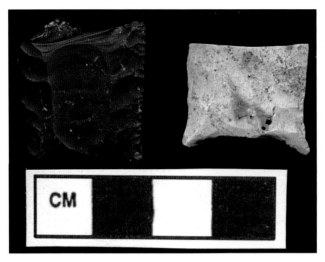

Folsom point bases from the MacHaffie Site —University of Montana Anthropology Collections

KING SITE

Isolated Folsom points—both fluted and unfluted varieties—have been found across Montana, including two at the King Site in the East Gallatin River valley near Bozeman. As reported by Matt Root and Leslie Davis in 2006, the site yielded an extensive array of projectile points, including a fluted point preform and a broken unfluted point. Both were manufactured of Madison chert from central Montana.

AGATE BASIN SITE

Excavations by George Frison and his University of Wyoming colleagues at the Agate Basin Site in Wyoming yielded abundant artifacts from the Folsom Culture. Agate Basin is located in far eastern Wyoming, just west of the Black Hills and approximately 100 miles south of the Montana state line. The site is located on the edge of a dry streambed that Folsom hunters used as a trap for nine bison. They killed the bison in winter and processed them into cache piles. In addition to bison, the hunters killed pronghorn, dog, rabbit, elk, and assorted small game at the site. The Agate Basin bison kill site yielded radiocarbon dates of approximately 10,690 years ago. Environmental data indicate a grassland dominated by short- and mixed-grass prairie, common to the area today.

The team from Wyoming recovered abundant tools, including an antler fluting tool, a bone needle, and a serrated bone scraper. The site also yielded more than 120 channel flakes and numerous Folsom points, as well as numerous endscrapers, suggestive of an array of on-site activities. While most of the stone materials at the site were procured locally, a few were exotics, including porcellanite from southeastern Montana and Knife River Flint from North Dakota. The wide array of activities represented at the site may indicate that multiple families or small bands gathered here to prepare for the oncoming winter, as was common among later Great Plains tribes.

BIG BLACK AND BOBTAIL WOLF SITES

Large Folsom occupations occur at the Big Black and Bobtail Wolf sites at the Knife River Flint Quarries in western North Dakota. At the Bobtail Wolf Site, researchers have found worn-out Folsom points made of Knife River Flint. The points must have been made at the flint quarries, extensively used by hunters, then carried by Folsom hunters returning to the site. Travel away from the site could have been quite local, perhaps just to Rainy Buttes and back, but it could also have covered long distances.

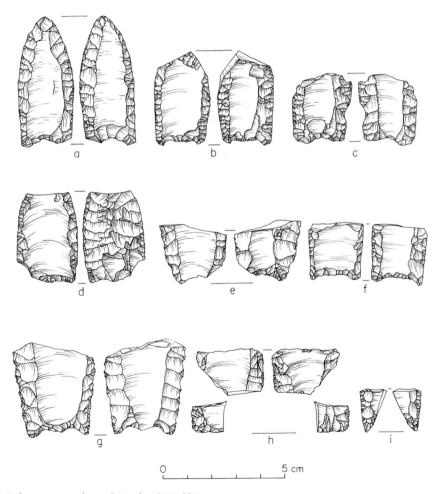

Folsom points from the Bobtail Wolf Site —Courtesy of Matthew J. Root; Sarah Moore illustration

It is clear that individuals collected Knife River Flint and produced tools that they carried with them on their travels.

In the southern area of Bobtail Wolf is a probable hearth with a concentration of burned Knife River Flint flaking debris. Here, individuals produced bifaces and Folsom points made not only of the locally abundant Knife River Flint but also of nonlocal porcellanite and Rainy Buttes silicified wood from about 60 miles to the south. In terms of Folsom mobility, 60 miles is small-scale. Sites such as Hell Gap, Lindenmeier, and Indian Creek held tools made from stone sourced as far as 300 miles away. The exotic stone at Indian Creek is from the Knife River Flint Quarries, evidence of cultural interactions with groups that used Bobtail Wolf. The Knife River Flint Quarries may have been an ideal location for regular social gatherings, with its abundance of high-quality stone, several watercourses, and likely large herds of bison.

Early Paleoindian sites to the south and southwest of the Knife River Flint Quarries have yielded flake tools, bifaces, and Folsom points made of Knife River Flint, supporting the notion that Folsom groups traveled from one region to another. Much of this travel was for subsistence, but a lot of it may have also been for socializing. Some archaeologists have suggested that large aggregations, as occur among most modern hunter-gatherers at some point in the year, probably did *not* occur for Folsom because of low populations. But does that mean that small-scale aggregation did not occur? Several authors, including Edwin Wilmsen, Doug Bamforth, and Jack Hofman, suggest that sites with different lithic raw materials in discrete work areas may indicate the conglomeration of individuals from disparate regions or, alternatively, individuals traveling large distances and returning with different types of stone.

If stone tools were traded, widely separated individuals needed to be able to reliably get together. Such small-scale aggregation would have been an avenue for people to maintain family relationships, trade for goods (including tool stone), dance, and find suitable mates. Such a pattern of aggregation for social reasons is seen among many hunter-gatherer groups worldwide. While population densities would have been low for Folsom peoples, such sparseness did not preclude social aggregation. On the contrary, such conditions would have made it beneficial for a few individuals, perhaps male hunters or a single household, to undertake long journeys for purely social reasons.

Travel from the Bobtail Wolf and Big Black sites in western North Dakota probably followed sources of permanent water, such as the Little Missouri, Missouri, and Cheyenne rivers. Half of all Folsom sites in the central and northern Great Plains are located adjacent to permanent sources of water, while another 41 percent are adjacent to seasonal lakes and playas or ephemeral streams. Water access was a key factor in the location of Folsom habitations.

Late Paleoindian Period

Agate Basin/Hell Gap Complex

Approximately 10,200 years ago, individuals ceased to use Folsom points in favor of Agate Basin and Hell Gap stemmed lanceolate points and, subsequently, a variety of other unfluted point types. It is important to remember that a change in technology does not necessarily mean there was a change in the identity of the people employing the technology. The Agate Basin and Hell Gap Complex, named for sites in Wyoming, existed mostly south of Montana and persisted until approximately 9,500 years ago. Although several Agate Basin– and Hell Gap–style points have been collected across Montana, suggesting a sizable human presence, few sites with Agate Basin/Hell Gap Complex artifacts have been studied in Montana. Among those few, Leslie Davis's Montana State University excavations at the KXGN-TV Site near Glendive in 1991 yielded three Hell Gap projectile points and numerous other stone tools.

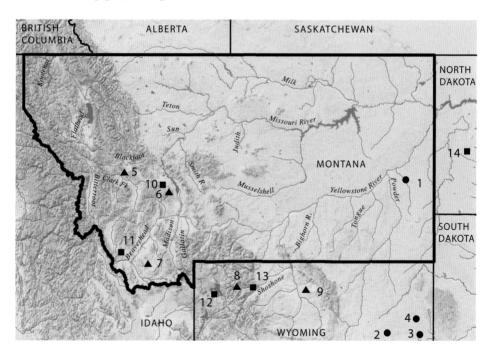

● AGATE BASIN/HELL GAP   ▲ FOOTHILL/MOUNTAIN   ■ CODY

1. KXGN-TV
2. Casper
3. Hell Gap
4. Agate Basin

5. Black Bear Coulee
6. Indian Creek
7. Barton Gulch
8. Mummy Cave
9. Medicine Lodge Creek
   (also Cody here)

10. MacHaffie
11. Mammoth Meadow
12. Osprey Beach
13. Horner
14. Benz

Late Paleoindian sites in Montana and the surrounding region

*Hell Gap (left) and
Agate Basin (right)
projectile points*

Agate Basin projectile points are elongated and lanceolate, with narrow, tapered bases and slightly convex blades. Hell Gap points are similar but typically have square stems. Both styles were produced using fine bifacial flaking, a technological descendant of Folsom. With the appearance of the lanceolate Agate Basin/Hell Gap points, it appears that Late Paleoindian hunters may have decided that the fluting of Folsom points was no longer worth the effort. Archaeologists know that Late Paleoindian projectile points were functionally useful and did not carry the same production costs as Folsom points, but because they don't know exactly why the Folsom fluted their points in the first place, they can't say why they stopped.

Most Late Paleoindian sites featuring bison remains have significantly higher counts of the animal than Folsom sites, which average a minimum of seven bison each. At the Agate Basin Site in Wyoming, the Folsom component yielded a minimum of nine bison and the Agate Basin–period (post-Folsom) component yielded a minimum of seventy-five bison.

Other Late Paleoindian sites show a similarly increasing intensity of bison hunting compared to sites of the Folsom period. For example, the Hell Gap components at the Casper Site in Wyoming yielded seventy-four bison, while the Hell Gap component at the Jones-Miller Site in Colorado yielded more than two hundred bison. Dating to the Late Paleoindian period (about 9,800 to 8,800 years ago), the Cody Complex bone bed at the Horner Site in Wyoming yielded at least fifty bison, while Cody Complex–period occupations at Olsen-Chubbuck in Colorado yielded several hundred animals. While certainly not a comprehensive analysis, this brief review of some important Late Paleoindian sites in the Great Plains indicates a real trend of increasing bison hunting intensity after Folsom.

Foothill/Mountain Complex

While few Agate Basin or Hell Gap Complex sites have been excavated in Montana, several sites in mountainous areas of the state have yielded Late Paleoindian artifacts that postdate Agate Basin/Hell Gap but feature somewhat similar projectile technology. This upland complex, known as Foothill/Mountain, may be culturally linked to those earlier cultural complexes but has slightly different technology due to the different prey types: bighorn sheep and pronghorn in the mountains compared to bison in the Great Plains.

BARTON GULCH SITE

The Barton Gulch Site along the Ruby River south of Virginia City, excavated by Leslie Davis and his colleagues from Montana State University in the 1980s, yielded abundant evidence of active use of uplands during the Late Paleoindian period, approximately 9,400 years ago. The hunter-gatherers at the site ate a variety of wild foods and left little

The Barton Gulch Site south of Virginia City

evidence of bison hunting. Game included deer, rabbit, hare, mink, and porcupine, while plants processed at the site included prickly pear cactus. Paleoindians processed this diverse suite of wild game and plants in more than eighty basin-shaped hearths and corresponding round roasting pits. Stone artifacts from the Barton Gulch Site resemble those of the Agate Basin cultural complex. Projectile points vary slightly and include concave bases, rather than the convex bases typical of Agate Basin–style projectiles.

BLACK BEAR COULEE SITE

The Black Bear Coulee Site, a few miles north of Drummond, yielded Agate Basin–like projectiles. HRA, an archaeological firm based in Missoula, was hired to excavate the site by the Montana Department of Transportation prior to a road-widening project between Drummond and Helmsville. The excavation yielded an extremely fruitful record of prehistoric use of the area, including evidence of diverse subsistence. See the chapter on the Early Plains Archaic period for more information about this site.

The Black Bear Coulee Site near Drummond

Steve Platt, archaeologist with the Montana Department of Transportation, at the Black Bear Coulee Site near Drummond. The Paleoindian occupations were in the layers below the white volcanic ash layer (center), which was from the eruption of Mount Mazama in Oregon, nearly 7,000 years ago.

MUMMY CAVE

One of the most important sites in the northwestern Great Plains is Mummy Cave, located along the North Fork of the Shoshone River next to U.S. Route 14, 12 miles east of the eastern entrance of Yellowstone National Park near Cody, Wyoming. The site is approximately 37 miles south of the Montana state line and provides an unparalleled record of early human use in the region. With more than thirty cultural horizons packed into 27 feet of stratigraphy, Mummy Cave is an outstanding record of nearly the entire early human history of the northern Rocky Mountains. It was excavated by Wilfred Husted and Robert Edgar in the 1960s. Mummy Cave has yielded radiocarbon dates of 9,230 years ago for its earliest occupations, which resemble those from Barton Gulch and Black Bear Coulee, probably Agate Basin/Hell Gap technology adapted to an upland lifestyle. Hunters of bighorn sheep utilized the cave during the entire span of its use. In the 1970s, George Frison recovered a net used to trap bighorn sheep from a nearby site in the Absaroka Mountains that dates to approximately 8,900 years ago.

Mummy Cave along the Shoshone River near Cody, Wyoming

Cody Complex

As with Agate Basin and Hell Gap, the Cody Complex is not well defined in Montana. It persisted in the northwestern Great Plains between 9,500 and 8,000 years ago. Cody sites generally are associated with bison hunting utilizing stemmed lanceolate projectile points, including Alberta, Eden, and Scottsbluff varieties. Each of these point styles is a cultural descendant of Agate Basin/Hell Gap point styles, as evidenced by fine bifacial flaking and the use of high-quality stone in their manufacture. Another characteristic attribute of Cody Complex sites is a beveled cutting tool called a Cody knife, one of the most interesting knife forms in the early human history of the Great Plains. The Cody knife is essentially an Alberta projectile point sharpened to an asymmetrical blade and is useful in bison processing and other cutting activities.

Several Cody buffalo kill sites in the Great Plains yielded large numbers of bison. The Hudson-Meng Site in far western Nebraska along the Wyoming state line yielded a minimum of four hundred bison killed during late fall to early winter approximately 9,400 years ago. Interestingly, the site lacked horns, suggesting the hunters collected and transported them away from the site. Hudson-Meng likely represents a substantial aggregation of between seventy-five and two hundred people, some from as far away as western North Dakota, as evidenced by Knife River Flint artifacts. The Olsen-Chubbuck Site, a similar site in eastern Colorado, yielded two hundred bison from a fall occupation, also dating to 9,400 years ago.

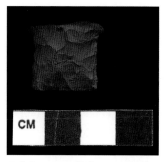

Cody knife from the Lake Lodge Meadow Site at Yellowstone Lake, Wyoming

While not well documented, Pictograph Cave near Billings contains a Late Paleoindian Cody occupation, as represented by this Cody point base from the site collection at the University of Montana.

MACHAFFIE SITE

A Montana site with a Cody Complex component is the MacHaffie Site near the small town of Montana City, approximately 7 miles southeast of Helena. The site is in an aspen and willow parkland on a terrace within the Helena (or Prickly Pear) valley, on a tributary of the Missouri River. The valley is bordered on the west by the Continental Divide and on the south, east, and north by the Big Belt Mountains, which effectively separate the site and the nearby Missouri River from the Great Plains to the east.

The Cody component, which overlies an older Folsom component, yielded a hearth with associated red ochre and stone tools. In his 1955 work on the site, Richard Forbis noted sixty stone tools, including six stemmed Scottsbluff points and a variety of scraping tools and bifaces. In her 1973 doctoral dissertation for Washington State University, Ruthann

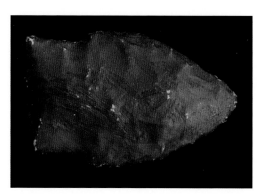

Cody projectile point found at the MacHaffie Site
—University of Montana Anthropology Collections

Knudson studied the Cody tools from the MacHaffie Site. She notes that most of the Cody Complex stone tools were produced from a locally available grayish white chalcedony, with a few produced from a fairly local reddish brown chert, and others possibly made of Knife River Flint. Knudson also analyzed all of the flaking debris from the Cody component, including an assemblage of 821 artifacts. Cody Complex stone toolmakers at the MacHaffie Site were focused on the production of bifaces, such as knives and projectile points, from local stone.

MAMMOTH MEADOW SITE

The Mammoth Meadow Site is one of only a few Cody Complex sites to be well excavated and reported in Montana. Excavated by Rob Bonnichsen of the University of Maine and later Oregon State University, this site is along a stream in Beaverhead County at an elevation of approximately 7,000 feet. The site yielded human hair and bison and other animal remains in association with radiocarbon dates of 9,400 years ago on a hearth and chert tool-manufacturing area. The site is located approximately 0.5 mile from the South Everson Creek chert quarries and was probably where hunters of the Late Paleoindian period made their tools from the chert.

The Mammoth Meadow Site on South Everson Creek west of Dillon

The Medicine Lodge Creek Site in the Bighorn Basin, Wyoming

MEDICINE LODGE CREEK SITE

An interesting site that has both Foothill/Mountain and Cody complex occupations—the only site discussed here that does—is the Medicine Lodge Creek Site on the western flanks of the Bighorn Mountains in north-central Wyoming. At an elevation of 4,800 feet, the Medicine Lodge Creek Site is located adjacent to a rock shelter on a beautiful spring-fed creek on the far eastern limits of the Bighorn Basin, within the transition zone between the hot, dry plains and the foothills and mountains. The shelter contains rock art from its much later Late Prehistoric occupations.

As outlined by George Frison and Danny Walker in their 2007 report, the Cody occupation occurs in level 18 of the site, dating to between 9,360 and 9,030 years ago and containing a prototypical stemmed Cody Complex point. Above this component is the Foothill/Mountain occupation, with a variety of projectile points similar to Agate Basin/Hell Gap and resembling points from Mummy Cave, Barton Gulch, and Black Bear Coulee. Radiocarbon dates of the Foothill/Mountain component range between 8,830 and 8,000 years ago. There are other archaeological sites in this area, suggesting a fairly continuous human presence through the Late Prehistoric period.

HORNER SITE

Several other sites in Wyoming have yielded substantial Cody Complex bison kill artifacts. The Horner Site in Cody, Wyoming, dates to approximately 9,100 years ago and yielded Alberta, Scottsbluff, and Eden projectile points. The site is on a bench of the Shoshone River north of town and yielded at least seventy bison, mostly cows killed in the late fall, possibly with the use of a corral at the river's edge.

OSPREY BEACH SITE

Another important Cody Complex site is Osprey Beach on Yellowstone Lake in Yellowstone National Park. With the exception of Mammoth Meadow in Montana, most Cody Complex sites are in the Great Plains. However, Osprey Beach is at an elevation of approximately 7,800 feet, indicating that Late Paleoindian people hunted more than just bison approximately 9,400 years ago. Protein residue on artifacts at the site

Excavations at the Osprey Beach Site
—Courtesy of Yellowstone National Park

A sandstone abrader found at Osprey Beach, probably used to smooth atlatl dart shafts. Sketches (top) of each side of the artifact (bottom) are shown.
—Courtesy of Yellowstone National Park

attest to a variety of game, including bear, deer, bighorn sheep, bison, and rabbit. Excavated by Brian Reeves of the archaeological consulting company Lifeways of Canada and Ann Johnson of Yellowstone National Park, the Osprey Beach Site contained stemmed Cody points of the Alberta and Scottsbluff varieties, Cody knives, sandstone abraders, and a variety of food-processing tools.

Obsidian from ten different sources has been recovered at Osprey Beach, not to mention cherts from a variety of sources across the region. The incredible diversity of stone materials speaks to wide-ranging travel and trade patterns during the Late Paleoindian period in the northern Rocky Mountain region.

Ann Johnson suggests that Cody Complex hunter-gatherers also exploited lake resources, perhaps with the use of skin boats. A stemmed Cody projectile point was recovered on Stevenson Island in Yellowstone Lake, indicating that Cody Complex individuals either had boats or were in Yellowstone during spring when the lake was still frozen and thus traversable. Hunter-gatherers were not likely to be in the high Yellowstone country during the winter because of the extremely difficult conditions. Individuals wintered in the lower valleys surrounding the park, entering the higher terrain only during the warmer seasons to obtain the wealth of natural resources available around the lake. Numerous Cody Complex artifacts have been found around Yellowstone Lake's perimeter.

BENZ SITE

Another Cody Complex site in close proximity to Montana is the Benz Site near the Knife River Flint Quarries in far western North Dakota. Matthew Root's work at this site yielded multiple occupations, including a well-dated Cody occupation. A radiocarbon date on hearth charcoal puts the Cody occupation at approximately 8,600 years ago. As with many other sites in the Knife River Flint Quarries, the Benz Site was a prolific stone workshop and quarry, with a single production concentration yielding nearly thirty-three thousand stone artifacts. Root suggests that Cody Complex hunter-gatherers traveled throughout eastern Montana from their base in the Knife River Flint Quarries in western North Dakota. Cody Complex sites in southern Saskatchewan suggest that inhabitants traveled there for bison hunting but then returned to their home turf—perhaps the Benz Site—in eastern Montana and western North Dakota.

Human Adaptation
during the Altithermal
←————————————————→
The Early Plains Archaic Period
8,000 TO 5,000 YEARS AGO

One of the hallmark characteristics of the Early Plains Archaic period from 8,000 to 5,000 years ago is a lack of well-excavated archaeological sites and an apparent decline in human population. Early Archaic sites are as rare as Paleoindian sites and are also less visible because the hunter-gatherers relied less on bison hunting. Large bison kill sites usually have lots of easily spotted bones. The Early Archaic period has yielded only one large bison kill site in the northern Great Plains, the Hawken Site in the Black Hills of Wyoming. Two other sites, the Licking Bison Site in South Dakota and Head-Smashed-In in Alberta, are small-scale bison kills in the Early Archaic period. Archaeologists think an emerging hot, dry climate called the Altithermal, or hypsithermal period, reduced the forage available to bison, so the bison population decreased. Bison teeth that date to the Early Archaic period are badly worn, suggesting dry grass and grit in their forage. Surface water may have been reduced during this time, and spring and summer seasons were warmer than during the preceding Late Paleoindian period. Hunter-gatherers were forced to adapt, finding other sources of food and relying less on large herds of bison.

The climatic changes are well documented by dozens of researchers. Analysis of fossil pollen shows evidence of changing plant communities, cores of lake sediment show evidence of increased wind and dust, and dunes show evidence of movement. Additional research in Saskatchewan shows heightened dune movements between approximately 8,000 and 4,000 years ago, suggesting increased aridity and high winds. My own research at Yellowstone National Park has shown increased aridity leading to an increase in grasslands in areas around Yellowstone Lake during the Early Archaic.

In 1958, William Mulloy was the first to suggest that humans may have abandoned the hot, dry, open plains in favor of uplands and water sources such as river valleys. He proposed this in part because Pictograph Cave near Billings, a site with a long history of occupation, lacks evidence of occupation during the Early Archaic. The clear decline in archaeological sites in the Great Plains between 8,000 and 5,000 years ago suggests

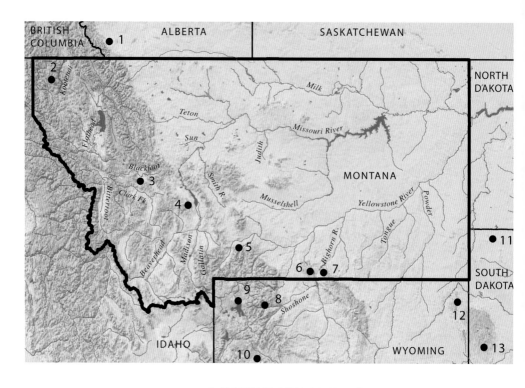

● EARLY PLAINS ARCHAIC

1. Head-Smashed-In
2. 24LN1054
3. Black Bear Coulee
4. Indian Creek
5. Myers-Hindman
6. Buckeye
7. Pretty Creek
8. Mummy Cave
9. Fishing Bridge Point
10. Helen Lookingbill
11. Licking
12. Hawken
13. Beaver Creek

Early Plains Archaic sites in Montana and the surrounding region

that Mulloy's abandonment theory may have some validity. In the southern Great Plains, David Meltzer has recorded archaeological sites with excavated wells, suggesting an extreme water shortage in that region.

Brian Reeves, among others, has disputed the abandonment theory, suggesting instead that the hot, dry conditions of the Altithermal resulted in less vegetation and therefore more erosion. The excess sediment accumulated in river valleys, so sites along streams were more likely to be deeply buried or eroded away. According to this theory, the lack of sites doesn't necessarily mean that populations decreased.

One of the most important long-term effects of the Altithermal was the extinction of the large bison specie, *Bison antiquus,* the only megafauna that survived the mass extinctions of 10,800 years ago. This large bison, along with the subspecies *Bison occidentalis,* failed to adapt to the hotter, dryer climate, but the modern, smaller species of bison—*Bison bison*—successfully emerged from these difficult times between 8,000 and 5,000 years ago. Animal extinctions occur only in extreme conditions, and the effects on humans were probably also severe. Humans adapted to the changing climate and decreasing bison by increasing the breadth of their diet, changing their technology, exploiting new resources, and living in different places.

In all likelihood, the decrease in bison hunting in the Early Archaic led to a decrease in group hunting. Individual hunting methods emerged, resulting in fewer large gatherings. Another major result of this transition from communal to individual hunting patterns was the switch to side-notched projectile points, which accompanied the adoption of the atlatl as the hunting weapon of choice. No longer did Great Plains and Rocky Mountain hunters produce the aesthetically pleasing projectile points of the Paleoindian period; instead they produced less elaborate points with side-notching to facilitate hafting. During the early portion of the Early Archaic, the side-notched points continued to be rather large and bifacially flaked.

While the atlatl was probably utilized prior to the Early Archaic, no clear archaeological evidence exists linking Paleoindian projectile points with atlatls. From dry rock shelters and caves of the Black Hills and Bighorn Mountains of Wyoming and Montana, archaeologits have recovered Archaic side-notched projectile points still hafted to their atlatl foreshafts, with the throwing boards and weights in direct association. Thus, the Early Archaic marks the first clear association of the atlatl with a specific style of projectile point.

Early Archaic point (left), Middle Archaic point (center), and Late Archaic point (right)

Another key trend of the Early Archaic period is the increased use of "site furniture," a term coined by the renowned American archaeologist Lewis Binford. Site furniture, such as a grinding stone used in the processing of seasonally available plants, is too large to transport from site to site. Hunter-gatherers left them behind at locations they knew they would use again.

One of the most innovative technologies of Early Archaic hunter-gatherers was the subterranean pit house. Archaeologists think that Paleoindians utilized portable hide structures for shelter, but hunter-gatherers of the Early Archaic excavated 6- to 9-foot-wide pits into the earth and erected wooden poles and covered them with hide. Evidence of these pit houses appears about 6,000 years ago, and their use escalated at the beginning of the Middle Archaic.

Pit houses are concentrated in east-central Wyoming but also have been excavated in southern Montana near the Wyoming border. Perhaps there are more yet-unfound pit houses in Montana. The pit houses are usually near plant resources and water, suggesting their association with the seasonal gathering of edible plants. They likely functioned as short-term residences and storage areas for hunter-gatherers moving into plant-collection areas in the spring and summer. The pit houses typically contain small, round storage features. The pit houses were also probably an ingenious solution to the increased heat of the Early Archaic period; it is cooler underground, after all. Because these pit houses were used more in the Middle Archaic, I discuss them in the next chapter.

The hunter-gatherers of the Early Archaic stuck close to their home territory, keeping their sites near water and within reach of known sources of game, edible plants, and stone. They made their stone tools from local stone—evidence that they weren't traveling far. Archaeologists call this a tethered settlement pattern, meaning the occupants moved only short distances—perhaps 20 to 40 miles—from their base.

SITE 24LN1054

Unnamed Site 24LN1054, on a high terrace along the Middle Kootenai River valley near Libby, shows extensive occupations during the Early and Middle Archaic periods. The site, which is now on the shore of Lake Koocanusa (a reservoir), was excavated by Alston Thoms of Washington State University's Center for Northwest Anthropology in the early 1980s. Thoms's team of archaeologists suggest that Site 24LN1054 functioned as a residential base during the winter. From the site, families ventured out to hunt and gather a wide variety of wild food in the Kootenai valley, but especially large game such as deer and elk. These animals dominate the remains found at the site, probably because the nearby south-facing slopes, with their increased forage and reduced snow cover, attracted browsing animals.

The presence of Early Archaic and other Archaic notched projectile points indicates that hunters camped at the site most extensively from 7,000 to 5,000 years ago. Artifacts recovered at the site include net weights used for trout fishing and pestles used to process root crops, which are abundant in the Kootenai valley. Unlike eastern Montana, the relatively cool and moist northwestern portion of Montana appeared to be largely unaffected by the hot, dry conditions of the Altithermal.

MYERS-HINDMAN SITE

The Myers-Hindman Site in Livingston is arguably the most important and one of the best-excavated Early Archaic sites in Montana. Excavated in the 1970s by Larry Lahren and colleagues, the site is located along the banks of the Yellowstone River, a stable source of water even during the hot, dry Altithermal. People living at Myers-Hindman exemplify the subsistence shifts that occurred between the Paleoindian and Early Archaic periods, when hunter-gatherers diversified their resource base. Bison hunting decreased between the Late Paleoindian occupation of about 9,000 years ago and the Early Archaic occupations of about 5,500 years ago, while procurement of other game increased substantially. Animal remains in the Early Archaic levels at Myers-Hindman include pronghorn, deer, elk, sheep, and dog.

The Myers-Hindman Site near Livingston

Early Archaic artifacts found at the site include side-notched points and numerous stone tools. Also found was a grinding stone—a large sandstone slab too large to carry during hunting and gathering forays. It was used for food processing at the site and was left in place to be used when people returned.

Larry Lahren showing colleagues the stratigraphy at the Myers-Hindman Site —Photo © 2006 by Larry Lahren

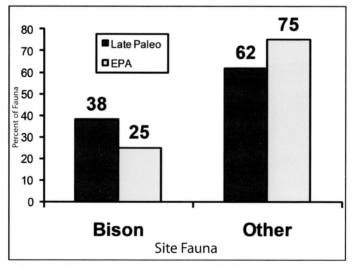

The use of bison decreased as the use of other prey increased at the Myers-Hindman Site between the Late Paleoindian and Early Plains Archaic periods. —Data from Lyman, 2004

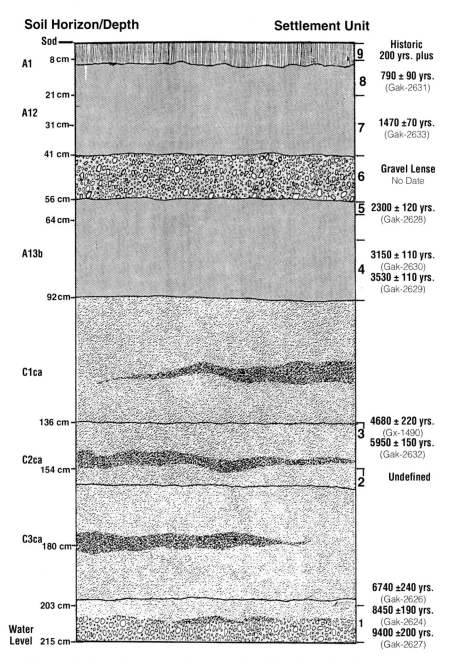

Soil Horizon/Depth

Sod
A1   8 cm
A12
   21 cm
   31 cm
   41 cm
   56 cm
   64 cm
A13b
   92 cm
C1ca
   136 cm
C2ca   154 cm
C3ca   180 cm
   203 cm
Water
Level   215 cm

Settlement Unit

9   Historic
     200 yrs. plus

8   790 ± 90 yrs.
     (Gak-2631)

7   1470 ±70 yrs.
     (Gak-2633)

6   Gravel Lense
     No Date

5   2300 ± 120 yrs.
     (Gak-2628)

4   3150 ± 110 yrs.
     (Gak-2630)
     3530 ± 110 yrs.
     (Gak-2629)

3   4680 ± 220 yrs.
     (Gx-1490)
     5950 ± 150 yrs.
     (Gak-2632)

2   Undefined

1   6740 ±240 yrs.
     (Gak-2626)
     8450 ±190 yrs.
     (Gak-2624)
     9400 ±200 yrs.
     (Gak-2627)

This sketch shows the excavated stratigraphy of the Myers-Hindman Site near Livingston. On the left side, soil layers are shown and labeled with A and C, extending down to the water table at a depth of 215 centimeters (7 feet). On the right side, the nine layers containing artifacts are labeled as settlement units. Uncalibrated dates are shown for the settlement units in which datable material such as charcoal was found. "Gak" indicates the dates were determined at the University of Georgia. —From Lahren, 2006

BLACK BEAR COULEE SITE

The Black Bear Coulee Site yielded two substantial Early Archaic occupations above its Paleoindian occupation. This site is located along springs and creeks just north of Drummond in the foothills of the Garnet Range at an elevation of about 4,000 feet. The first of the two Early Archaic occupations, dated to 7,000 years ago, is located immediately beneath a 6-inch layer of ash from the eruption of Mount Mazama in Oregon approximately 6,850 years ago. It is possible that Early Archaic peoples at the site lived through the dramatic eruption and were present to see the ash falling over the hills and streams of western Montana. The second occupation dates to about 6,700 years ago, soon after the eruption. The layer of ash seems to have had little long-term effect on the people of western Montana; Early Archaic peoples lived there before and after the eruption with equal success.

Stratigraphy at the Black Bear Coulee Site near Drummond. Early Archaic occupations were above and below the ash layer (white) erupted from Mount Mazama in Oregon.

BUCKEYE SITE

Another important Early Archaic occupation in Montana is the Buckeye Site in Kings Canyon near a permanent spring in Carbon County in south-central Montana. This site is approximately 2 miles west of the Pryor Mountains and 3.5 miles north of Warren, at an elevation of 4,680 feet. Ethnoscience, an archaeological consulting firm, excavated the site in the 1990s prior to the installation of an oil pipeline. Radiocarbon dates from the well-stratified site indicate three occupations around 6,300 years ago. Excavations yielded nearly two thousand stone artifacts, including one Early Archaic side-notched projectile point with traces of pronghorn blood. Mussel shell was also abundant at the site, suggesting its collection, probably from nearby Sage Creek; mussel was an important part of Early Archaic subsistence in south-central Montana.

Plant remains at the Buckeye Site indicate use of prickly pear cactus and biscuitroot for food, and sagebrush and pine for firewood. The pine probably came from the nearby Pryor Mountains.

PRETTY CREEK SITE

An Early Archaic site worthy of mention is Pretty Creek, also in Carbon County, in the south-central portion of the state. The site is located adjacent to a tributary of the Bighorn River in the foothills of the Pryor Mountains, approximately 6 miles north of the Wyoming state line in Bighorn Canyon National Recreation Area. Lawrence Loendorf and colleagues with the National Park Service excavated the site between 1973 and 1974. A radiocarbon date of approximately 7,750 years ago places its occupation in the early portion of the Early Archaic, making it a significant find.

HELEN LOOKINGBILL SITE

The Helen Lookingbill Site is located at an elevation of greater than 10,000 feet within the Absaroka Mountains of northwestern Wyoming. Excavated by Marcel Kornfeld, Mary Lou Larson, and colleagues from the University of Wyoming, the Helen Lookingbill Site is testament to the literal heights Early Archaic hunter-gatherers went to in order to survive in the hot, dry climate of the Altithermal. The archaeologists recovered remains of seven male deer from a bone bed dating to approximately 6,800 years ago. Several bighorn sheep are represented at the site, but no bison. Local cherts were quarried at the site, suggesting a tethered settlement pattern around known resources in this rugged setting.

MUMMY CAVE

Mummy Cave in northern Wyoming, among the most important Early Archaic sites anywhere, yielded five substantial Early Archaic occupations between approximately 7,700 and 5,600 years ago. Large side-notched

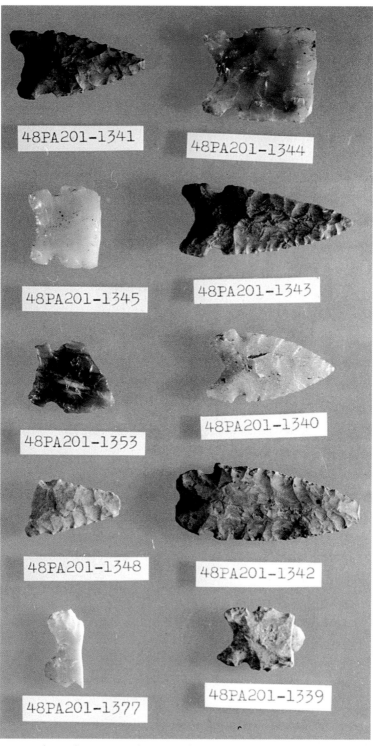

48PA201-1341

48PA201-1344

48PA201-1345

48PA201-1343

48PA201-1353

48PA201-1340

48PA201-1348

48PA201-1342

48PA201-1377

48PA201-1339

Early Archaic projectile points from Mummy Cave —Courtesy of
Buffalo Bill Historical Center, Cody, Wyoming; gift of Harold McCracken, Mummy
Cave Collection; Jack Richard photo; PN.29.48PA201-L21

Mummy Cave, the dark area at the base of the tall cliff above the river in distance, along the Shoshone River —Courtesy of Buffalo Bill Historical Center, Cody, Wyoming; Gift of Harold McCracken, Mummy Cave Collection; Jack Richard photo; PN.29.001

projectile points characterize the three main occupations of 7,700, 7,200, and 5,700 years ago. In each of the occupations, the animal bones notably lack one key ingredient: bison. Bighorn sheep is dominant, along with lesser remains of deer, elk, marmot, and birds. The Early Archaic occupations contained ten basin-shaped fire hearths and thirty-two Early Archaic side-notched projectile points. Numerous scraping tools and knives were recovered, as was a bone needle and a piece of red ochre that was probably used for art, ceremony, or decoration.

HAWKEN SITE

The only Early Archaic bison kill found to date in Montana or Wyoming is the Hawken Site in the Black Hills of Wyoming. George Frison excavated the site in the 1980s, finding at least one hundred individual male *Bison occidentalis* (now extinct) in an arroyo. The bison were killed in winter. Dozens of side-notched Early Plains Archaic projectile points were recovered at the site. Extensive processing of the bison carcasses may indicate that the hunters realized they needed to maximize their yield from this rare bison kill. Climatic data obtained from bison remains at the site indicate a wetter climate than might be expected for the Altithermal. This may suggest that the particular season of the Hawken kill was wetter than typical, without necessarily saying anything about the long-term trends of the hotter, drier climate so common to the Early Archaic.

LICKING BISON SITE

In addition to the Hawken Site in Wyoming, the Licking Bison Site in South Dakota is one of the few bison kill sites in the northern Great Plains that dates to the Early Archaic period. The Licking Bison Site is located in Harding County in the northwestern corner of the state, less than 20 miles from the southeasternmost corner of Montana. It is along Graves Creek, a small feeder stream of the South Fork Grand River. A variety of Early Archaic side-notched projectile points were recovered at the Licking Bison Site, all of which match similar specimens from Mummy Cave and the Hawken Site in nearby Wyoming. Bones from the bison kill were radiocarbon dated to between 6,730 and 6,410 years ago.

Hunters drove the animals into a gully, or arroyo, about 3 to 5 feet wide and 2 to 3 feet deep. The South Dakota Archaeological Resource Center excavated completely articulated bison skeletons in the southwestern corner of the Licking Bison Site, suggesting that the animals were not processed after the kill event. In the eastern portion of the site, bison skeletons appear to have been cut in half by prehistoric butchers, while to the north, the bison were further separated into smaller parts associated with burned bone and a small hearth.

BEAVER CREEK SHELTER

Beaver Creek Shelter, a rock shelter within Wind Cave National Park, is a few miles southeast of the small town of Pringle, South Dakota, and approximately 20 miles south of the Black Hills area. The site is located within an eroding Madison Limestone outcrop near Beaver Creek, a tributary of the Cheyenne River. Excavations in the deeper levels of the site yielded an Early Archaic occupation with radiocarbon dates of between 6,700 and 6,200 years ago and an associated side-notched projectile point. Among the animal remains from the site are a variety of frogs and reptiles, suggesting that the arid conditions of the Altithermal had not dried out this north-facing rock shelter. In addition, remains of deer, bison, and pronghorn indicate a diverse diet for Early Archaic hunter-gatherers at the site.

HEAD-SMASHED-IN BUFFALO JUMP

Among the more important bison kill sites in the northern Great Plains is the Head-Smashed-In Buffalo Jump just north of the Oldman River in southern Alberta. While the Early Archaic site occupation was very small, it was the first at this bison kill site. Brian Reeves notes that the site yielded a small contingent of Early Archaic projectile points produced mostly from local quartzite but featuring a few exotics. As at other Early Archaic sites, the local stone suggests that Early Archaic hunter-gatherers operated within a specific territory with access to known resources.

EARLY HUNTING TRADITION

Two incised outlines of animal figures at Legend Rock in Wyoming have been dated to more than 6,000 years ago. These are the oldest well-dated rock art images in the region. Animal figures of the same type have been identified at other sites, including in Montana. This early rock art, in a style called the Early Hunting Tradition, focused on the depiction of hunted animals, such as bison, elk, sheep, and deer. These fairly realistic images are usually pecked into rock faces. Abstract images became much more common in the Late Plains Archaic period.

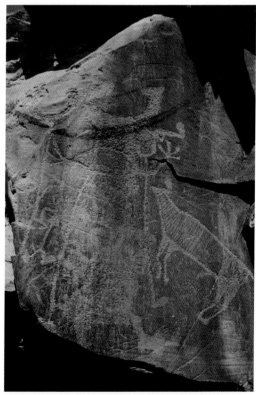

Archaic rock art at Legend Rock near Thermopolis, Wyoming

FISHING BRIDGE POINT SITE

An increase in the number of Early Archaic occupations in upland areas would support the hypothesis that hunter-gatherers of this time period at least partially abandoned the hot, open plains for the cooler mountains. Therefore, it is somewhat surprising that high-elevation locations like Yellowstone National Park in south-central Montana and northwestern Wyoming have few well-documented Early Archaic sites. Nonetheless, Fishing Bridge Point Site, along the northwestern shore of Yellowstone Lake, contains a small Early Archaic component. Excavations by the University of Montana in 2009 unearthed a large obsidian blade tool and other stone debris near a small basin-shaped hearth feature with a radiocarbon date of 5,870 years. The blade tool shows extensive wear and has been sharpened on its distal tip and lateral edges, suggesting it was used as a multipurpose cutting and scraping tool. Analysis of blood protein on its edges indicated that it had been used to butcher a deer. X-ray fluorescence analysis of the obsidian shows it was obtained from nearby Obsidian Cliff, approximately 20 miles northwest of the site. The presence of Early Archaic sites on the Yellowstone Plateau shows that Early Archaic hunter-gatherers moved into the uplands, at least during the warmer months, to hunt animals and collect the plethora of plant resources available around the shores of Yellowstone Lake.

The Fishing Bridge Point Site at Yellowstone Lake in Wyoming

*Early Archaic
obsidian blade/
scraper from the
Fishing Bridge
Point Site in
Yellowstone
National Park*

*Early Archaic
hearth at the
Fishing Bridge
Point Site
excavation at
Yellowstone
Lake,
Wyoming*

A Time of Transition

The Middle Plains Archaic Period

5,000 TO 3,000 YEARS AGO

The Middle Plains Archaic period was a time of transition from the diversified subsistence of the Early Plains Archaic to full-scale bison hunting of the Late Plains Archaic. Hunter-gatherers continued the trends begun during the Early Plains Archaic, including diversification of the food base, use of site furniture, and heightened use of foothills and mountains. Between 5,000 and 4,000 years ago, they increased their use of subterranean pit houses in eastern Montana and western Wyoming and continued active habitation of northwestern Montana along the Kootenai, Flathead, Clark Fork, and Blackfoot rivers. By the end of the period—between approximately 4,000 and 3,000 years ago—many hunter-gatherers began to transition back to a Great Plains bison hunting culture, a tradition linked with the emergence of substantial *Bison bison* herds in the northern Great Plains. The hot, dry climate of the Altithermal began to gradually dissipate, with slightly cooler temperatures and increasing precipitation returning to the Great Plains. This period of climatic transition was labeled the Medithermal by renowned climatologist Ernst Antevs, whose analysis of worldwide pollen records shows a cooler and wetter trend emerging approximately 4,500 years ago. The Blytt-Sernander climatic sequence dubs this climactic period the Subboreal and places it between approximately 5,000 and 2,500 years ago. The cooler, wetter climate led to increased grasslands and larger herds of bison.

With the exception of increasing bison use, subsistence patterns appear to represent continuity between the Early and Middle Archaic in Montana. Most Middle Archaic sites yield a diverse array of foods, some including bison, others not. Deer, pronghorn, bighorn sheep, small mammals, and even insects were important foods.

The number of sites increases all over the northern Great Plains during the Middle Plains Archaic, with most states seeing approximately 25 to 50 percent increases over the Early Plains Archaic. George Frison's study of the northwestern Great Plains shows a substantial increase in datable components beginning approximately 5,500 to 5,000 years ago, a trend that continues through the Middle Plains Archaic. In Yellowstone National Park, Paul Sanders counted twenty-four Middle Archaic sites versus only fourteen Early Archaic. Because these data are largely for a mountainous area, they may indicate an overall population increase. If people had simply moved back into the Great Plains, site counts may not have increased in the uplands. Alternatively, with less time elapsed between the Middle Archaic and the present, it may just be that more such sites have survived erosion or sediment burial.

In Yellowstone National Park, the number of sites increased in the Gardiner Basin (north of Gardiner along the Yellowstone River), where elevations are the lowest in the park, averaging about 5,000 feet above mean sea level. You'd expect fewer sites here during the Early Archaic if hunter-gatherers were seeking cooler uplands during the Altithermal. However, many hunter-gatherers continued to use the upland areas during the Middle Archaic as well.

The Yellowstone River valley and its tributaries—including the Powder and Tongue rivers—contain nine of the twelve important Middle Plains Archaic sites in Montana. Pictograph Cave, Myers-Hindman, Rigler Bluffs, and Airport Rings are within the Yellowstone valley between

Middle Archaic Site	Bison	Deer	Pronghorn	Bighorn Sheep	Small Mammals	Plants/ Insects
24LN2210, Kootenai River, MT	X	**X**				
Sun River, MT	**X**	X	**X**		X	X
Myers-Hindman, MT	X		X	**X**		
Spiro, MT	X	X	X	X	**X**	X
Buckeye, MT			**X**		X	X
Kobold, MT	X					
Cactus Flower, AB	**X**	X	X		X	X
Long Creek, SK	X					
Lightning Spring, SD	X		**X**		X	
Beaver Creek Shelter, SD	X	X	X			
McKean, WY	**X**	X	X		X	X
Leigh Cave, WY						X
Medicine Lodge Creek, WY	X	X		X	X	X
Dead Indian Creek, WY		**X**	X	X		
Mummy Cave, WY			X	**X**	X	X

Summary of animal remains found at fifteen Middle Archaic sites in Montana and the surrounding region. X indicates that those animals were present; a bold X indicates that particular animal dominated the bone assemblage.

Gardiner and Billings, while five others are on Yellowstone River tributaries. Although Middle Archaic bifurcate projectile points have been found at Pictograph Cave and nearby Ghost Cave, it is difficult to associate the artifacts with specific site occupations.

Oxbow and McKean Points

Middle Plains Archaic hunters utilized Oxbow and McKean projectile points, among other varieties—including Duncan, Hanna, and Mallory. These points are bifurcates, meaning they have indented, or concave, bases. Following George Frison, I agree that the latter three varieties are morphological varieties of Oxbow and McKean points. Oxbow and McKean points are more or less identical point varieties from the Middle Archaic period and do not represent a sequence in point technology.

The three most common varieties of Middle Archaic projectile points: Oxbow (left), McKean notched (center), and McKean lanceolate (right). The McKean lanceolate at right is about 35 millimeters long.

In general, Oxbow points are smaller, squat versions of the larger, lanceolate McKean points. Middle Archaic projectile points typically range in size between 30 and 50 millimeters long and 10 to 25 millimeters wide, with the smaller Oxbow points averaging 20 to 35 millimeters long and 8 to 15 millimeters wide.

George Frison suggested that point size should not be considered a significant variable in projectile points, since size diminishes with use of the point. In other words, brand-new McKean projectile points will, over the course of their lives, get worn down to smaller, older McKean projectile points. It is conceivable that with extended use and retouching, McKean points become Oxbow points. The same people likely used both varieties (big McKean points and smaller Oxbow points) depending on the condition of their stone tool kit.

Typical McKean projectile points are lanceolate with convex to straight blades. The point blades can be serrated or not, with the latter most common. McKean points tend to have elongated, bifurcate bases compared to the smaller Oxbow points, while both McKean and Oxbow points have a concave indentation on the base that resembles a notch. Very often, but not always, McKean points will also have side notches.

Middle Archaic projectile point from Pictograph Cave near Billings. Point is about 3 centimeters wide.
—Courtesy of Montana State Parks, a division of Montana Fish, Wildlife, and Parks

The McKean points with side notches could be characterized as tri-notch, although that is not a common way of referring to such points. More commonly, "tri-notch" refers to very small Late Prehistoric arrow points with basal and side notches. Similar projectile points in eastern North American are called bifurcate points.

Oxbow points, because of their smaller size, are not characterized as lanceolate, like the larger McKean points. However, Oxbow points carry virtually all of the other morphological characteristics of McKean points, including bifurcate bases, frequent side notches, and occasional serration of convex blades. It would lessen the confusion if all McKean/Oxbow projectile points were given one name, because they are virtually identical points utilized between 5,000 and 3,000 years ago. Distinguishing between them implies use by different cultures when, in fact, there is little evidence that this is true.

There appears also to be a regional preference in point identification by archaeologists. Oxbow is the name used for Middle Archaic bifurcate projectile points in northern Montana and southern Canada, while McKean is used for similar points in southern Montana, Wyoming, and the Dakotas. However, some researchers have identified McKean sites in Canada, while others have identified Oxbow sites in Wyoming. Thus, whether an archaeologist calls a Middle Archaic bifurcate projectile point an Oxbow or a McKean (or even a Duncan, Hanna, or some other name) appears to be a somewhat idiosyncratic decision.

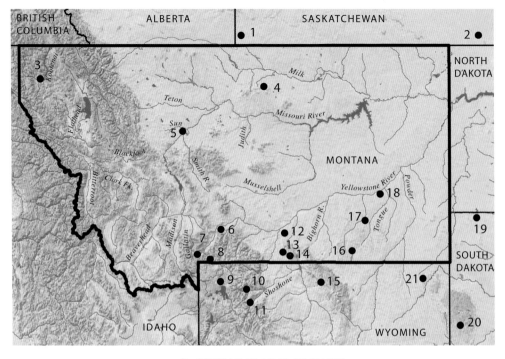

● MIDDLE PLAINS ARCHAIC

1. Cactus Flower
2. Long Creek
3. 24LN2210
4. 24HL1215
5. Sun River
6. Myers-Hindman
7. Rigler Bluffs
8. Airport Rings
9. Fishing Bridge Point
10. Mummy Cave
11. Dead Indian Creek
12. Pictograph Cave
13. Spiro
14. Buckeye
15. Medicine Lodge Creek/
    Leigh Cave
16. Kobold
17. Dodge
18. Powers-Yonkee
19. Lightning Spring
20. Beaver Creek Shelter
21. McKean

Middle Plains Archaic Sites in Montana and the surrounding area

Middle Plains Archaic Sites in Montana

SITE 24LN2210

In far northwestern Montana on the Kootenai River, archaeological consultants HRA, based in Missoula, completed excavations at unnamed Site 24LN2210 prior to replacement of the electric transmission line that runs between Libby in Lincoln County and Bonner's Ferry in Idaho. The site, which yielded a Middle Archaic occupation dating to between 5,150 and 4,760 years ago, shows repeated use of the Kootenai River valley for deer hunting. Animal remains at the site indicate that it was probably a fall hunting camp. Kootenai use of the site began approximately 5,000 years ago and continued unabated until European-American contact. Kootenai hunters processed deer at the site and then cooked the meat in roasting pits, sometimes lined with bark.

Although hunters obtained most of their stone materials locally within the Kootenai River valley and surrounding region, X-ray fluorescence analysis of three obsidian artifacts showed they were from far-away sources. Two were from Whitewater Ridge in northeastern Oregon, and the other was from Bear Gulch on the Montana-Idaho border southwest of Dillon, Montana. These stone sources suggest that although the Kootenai hunters spent most of their time in the Kootenai valley of northwestern Montana, trade and travel took them southward through the Bitterroot valley and westward across the Columbia Plateau to Oregon.

SUN RIVER SITE

One of the most important and informative Middle Plains Archaic sites in Montana is west of Great Falls in the floodplain of the Sun River, a major tributary of the Missouri River, at an elevation of approximately 3,225 feet. HRA excavated the Sun River Site prior to construction of a levee by the United States Army Corps of Engineers. Under the direction of Sally Greiser and T. Weber Greiser, HRA identified at least six occupations dating to between 5,200 and 2,800 years ago. The three major Sun River occupations span the entire Middle Archaic period, including cultural level VI at 5,200 years ago, cultural level V at 4,500 years ago, and

Excavations at the Sun River Site
—Courtesy of HRA

cultural level IV at 3,500 years ago. Each of these occupations yielded Oxbow projectile points in association with animal and stone remains, as well as cultural features, such as fire pits and work areas.

Based on analysis of animal remains from the site, each of the major Middle Archaic occupations was during the fall and was probably composed of approximately twenty-five people for a few days at a time. The animal remains reflect the gradual transition to bison hunting that occurred over the course of the Middle Archaic period, especially for those people living east of the Continental Divide. Pronghorn remains dominate the earliest site occupations, but bison dominate the later site occupations.

During the earliest occupation at Sun River, about 5,200 years ago, the occupants utilized a wide array of locally available fauna, including a minimum of four individual pronghorn, which accounted for 78 percent of the identifiable remains. Other animals represented include birds, deer, bison, jackrabbit, and wolf. Cultural features include a bone-processing area and a hearth, probably used in the cooking of processed game.

In the middle occupation, dated to 4,500 years ago, hunter-gatherers once again conducted a diverse suite of activities but appear to have switched their diet to one based predominantly on bison. A minimum number of six bison accounted for 66 percent of the identifiable remains. At least one pronghorn was used by site occupants, making up 20 percent of the identifiable animal remains. Other animals represented in the middle site occupation include elk, deer, birds, and shellfish.

In the final Middle Archaic occupation, dated to 3,500 years ago, a minimum of three bison composed more than 93 percent of the identifiable

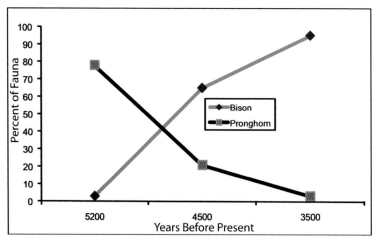

Bison use increased and pronghorn use decreased during the three Middle Archaic occupations at Sun River. —Data from Greiser and others,

remains. Other animal remains accounted for less than 1 percent of the total bone assemblage and included a minor amount of pronghorn, fox, shellfish, rabbit, and fish.

HRA also completed a detailed analysis of pollen remains from the site, concluding that increasing moisture and decreasing temperatures resulted in an increase in pine in the area between 5,200 and 3,000 years ago. During the hot, dry Altithermal at the beginning of the Middle Archaic, pine pollen counts were low, but cooler, wetter conditions fostered the expansion of pine in nearby uplands and the expansion of short-grass prairie habitat, thus increasing bison herds in Montana's Great Plains.

Another interesting trend at Sun River is the consistent use of locally available stone for toolmaking. While the types of animals hunted underwent a transition at the site, stone procurement patterns did not change. It is possible that the hunter-gatherers still traveled to find bison herds, but if they did, it seems odd that they didn't take advantage of other sources of stone. Most likely, bison populations rebounded enough locally that individuals did not have to travel very far for their subsistence activities.

SITE 24HL1215

Another site in the northern tier of Montana is unnamed Site 24HL1215, at an elevation of approximately 4,680 feet in the Bear Paw Mountains south of Havre. In 2006–2007 under the direction of Anna Prentiss and Robert O'Boyle, a team from the University of Montana excavated a small Middle Archaic component at the site. The earliest occupation was

Excavation of a grid of 1-meter-square plots by the University of Montana at Site 24HL1215 in the Bear Paw Mountains —Anna Prentiss photo

approximately 5,500 years ago and is associated with Middle Archaic Oxbow projectile points—one of the earliest sites with Oxbow points in the region. The small occupation, perhaps a group of hunters, used the uplands of the Bear Paw Mountains for hunting and gathering. The production and use of bifacial and unifacial tools centered around the hearths, suggesting to researchers that the occupation may have been within a shelter of some kind. While site occupants used a variety of local stone, they also carried exotic stone with them, including Knife River Flint from western North Dakota and obsidian from Yellowstone National Park.

MYERS-HINDMAN SITE

The Myers-Hindman Site along the Yellowstone River in Livingston yielded a substantial Middle Archaic component in addition to its Late Paleoindian and Early Archaic occupations. Careful excavation by Larry Lahren resulted in an excellent understanding of the subsistence and settlement patterns of site inhabitants. In contrast to Sun River, there is virtually no change in the composition of animal remains between the Early Archaic occupations of 5,300 years ago and the Middle Archaic occupations of 3,300 years ago. In the Early and Middle Archaic occupations, bighorn sheep account for 37.5 and 34.5 percent of the total identifiable animal assemblage, respectively, while bison account for only 18.8 and 12.5 percent. The big differences between Sun River and Myers-Hindman are elevation and topographic position. Sun River was probably a late-fall camp in a comparatively low-elevation river valley (about 3,000 feet), with hunting aimed at locally available game, including mostly bison and pronghorn. In contrast, Myers-Hindman is a comparatively high-elevation site above 5,000 feet in the foothills of the Absaroka Mountains. The site was likely a special-purpose location for hunting bighorn sheep, and similar in many ways to Mummy Cave on the opposite side of the range in Wyoming.

RIGLER BLUFFS SITE

The Rigler Bluffs Site is located on the southern bank of the Yellowstone River where it meanders east-west through the small community of Corwin Springs south of Livingston. Although Rigler Bluffs has had significantly less-intensive excavations than the Myers-Hindman Site, Aubrey Haines has collected charcoal from a heavily used hearth feature eroding out of the riverbank at the site. The feature measured more than 30 inches across and was lined with rocks, suggesting that perhaps it was a game-roasting pit. Two radiocarbon dates indicate a Middle Archaic occupation between 5,040 and 4,900 years ago. The lone diagnostic artifact at the site was the base of an obsidian McKean projectile point found within one of the hearths.

The Rigler Bluffs Site along the Yellowstone River near Corwin Springs
—Yellowstone National Park photo

AIRPORT RINGS SITE

At the Airport Rings Site along the Yellowstone River near Gardiner, the University of Montana excavated a Middle Archaic hearth in the northeastern corner of a stone circle. The more or less circular hearth measured approximately 25 inches wide and 10 inches deep. It was densely packed with fire-cracked rock and very small charcoal fragments and occasional bone. None of the bone was identifiable by species, but its presence suggests that the hearth was used for processing food. Analysis of pollen from the hearth indicates that people processed wild lettuce and other plants as well.

Based on the radiocarbon date of approximately 4,500 years ago, the hearth may indicate the earliest known use of a stone circle anywhere in the region. Stone circles, which indicate the use of a tepee, generally postdate the Middle Archaic, but a few have been dated to approximately 4,000 to 3,000 years ago. Thus, it is not completely out of the question that Middle Archaic hunter-gatherers built a stone circle with an interior hearth along the Yellowstone River 4,500 years ago.

Stone artifacts in and around the hearth suggest that one or more people sat at the fire roasting game and making hunting equipment. The most common stone in the assemblage was obsidian from Obsidian Cliff, approximately 20 miles to the south. Chert from the Crescent Hill Formation near Mammoth Hot Springs was also common. Diagnostic

Excavation of the Airport Rings Site near Gardiner by the University of Montana in 2008

A hearth at the Airport Rings Site near Gardiner

projectile points include a Middle Archaic Oxbow point base produced from Obsidian Cliff obsidian.

SPIRO SITE

The Spiro Site features the only well-excavated pit house in Montana. Pit houses, circular subterranean pits that may have been covered by structures, were used during the Early to Middle Archaic transition by hunter-gatherers in the northern Great Plains. The vast majority of these features have been found in the very hot, dry portions of east-central Wyoming and northern Utah, indicating that they are a possible adaptation to arid conditions. The Spiro Site, situated in the northernmost portion of the Bighorn Basin in one of the hottest portions of Montana, supports this theory. The site is on a slope overlooking Sage Creek, a small tributary of the Clarks Fork Yellowstone River.

Excavation of the Spiro Site by Ethnoscience
—Courtesy of Ethnoscience

Cross section of a Middle Archaic pit house at the Spiro Site
—Courtesy of Ethnoscience

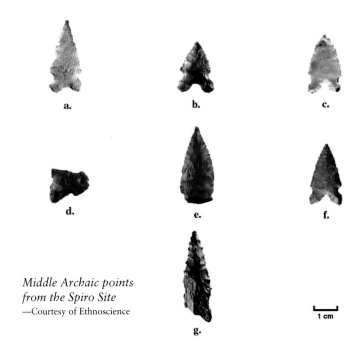

a.   b.   c.

d.   e.   f.

*Middle Archaic points
from the Spiro Site*
—Courtesy of Ethnoscience

1 cm

g.

Ethnoscience of Billings conducted excavations at the site due to the imminent construction of an oil pipeline between Alberta and Wyoming in 1997. Excavation at the Spiro Site yielded an intensive Middle Archaic occupation, characterized most importantly by the presence of nine pit houses dating to between 4,050 and 3,600 years ago. Thirteen cultural features, including shallow basins, ovens, and hearths, provided additional dates to corroborate this period of occupation.

The pit houses measure between 5 and 15 feet in diameter and range in depth from 10 to 20 inches below the ground surface. Earth ovens and hearths were common both inside and outside of the pit houses; however, no post molds or storage pit features were identified at the site, making these pit houses somewhat distinct from those at sites to the south in Wyoming.

Animal remains indicate a diverse diet at the Spiro Site, including rabbit, deer, sheep, and bison. While the latter two were rare at the site, rabbit was very common. A variety of stone tools were recovered, including bifaces, scraping tools, and nine McKean/Oxbow bifurcate projectile points. The stone, including silicified sediment, quartzite, basalt, chert, and porcellanite, was largely obtained near the site. A variety of bone and antler tools were found at the site, including a coyote skull in a basin feature, bone awls, and bone beads. The beads were cut from the narrow, hollow, long bones of rabbit and other small game. Sagebrush was the primary fuel used in the fire hearths, while goosefoot, prickly pear cactus, and sunflowers were all collected and eaten by hunter-gatherers at the site.

The Spiro Site is important because it indicates that the Early Archaic pattern of subsistence continued well into the Middle Archaic period. While bison had regained prominence at the Sun River Site and bighorn sheep were the focus at Myers-Hindman, hunter-gatherers at Spiro exploited a wide variety of small- and medium-sized game.

BUCKEYE SITE

Another site that suggests continuity between the Early and Middle Archaic periods is the Buckeye Site on the northern edge of the Bighorn Basin in south-central Montana. Excavated along with the nearby Spiro Site by Ethnoscience and Lynelle Peterson as part of the pipeline project, the Buckeye Site yielded two Middle Plains Archaic occupations dating to between approximately 4,450 and 4,100 years ago. Middle Archaic site occupants utilized three hearths at the site, burning sagebrush, greasewood, and pine. They hunted pronghorn and gathered freshwater mussels and prickly pear cactus, suggesting a diverse subsistence much like that identified at Spiro.

KOBOLD SITE

The Kobold Site is located in Big Horn County along Rosebud Creek, which flows southeasterly to its confluence with the Tongue River near Decker. In 1970, George Frison reported that this site contained the earliest buffalo jump that postdates the Altithermal. We now know the earliest record of buffalo jumping in the region was a small episode at Head-Smashed-In in southern Alberta during the Early Archaic period, about 5,700 years ago. The Kobold Site represents the earliest evidence of buffalo jumping in Montana, dating to approximately 4,000 years ago based on the projectile point style, though no radiocarbon dates have been assayed.

The Kobold Site is located directly beneath an approximately 25-foot-high sandstone escarpment, ideal for buffalo jumping. The Middle Archaic component of the site yielded a minimum of sixty-five bison, as well as thirty-three projectile points, predominantly of the Middle Archaic McKean variety. Several retouched flakes used in the butchery of bison were also found, as well as one shell bead.

POWERS-YONKEE AND DODGE SITES

Two additional Middle Archaic sites in southeastern Montana are the Powers-Yonkee Site, located near the confluence of the Tongue and Yellowstone rivers in Prairie County, and the Dodge Site, located on a feeder stream of the Tongue River in Rosebud County. While not reported completely, both sites yielded bifurcate projectile points. According to Leslie Davis of Montana State University, the Dodge Site, with at least four McKean lanceolate points, is a probable cache location.

McKean-like points that George Frison suggests are better attributed to the Late Archaic period are associated with a 3,100-year-old date for Powers-Yonkee.

Middle Plains Archaic Sites outside Montana

CACTUS FLOWER SITE

The Cactus Flower Site is located on a terrace of the South Saskatchewan River west of Medicine Hat, Alberta, approximately 75 miles north of the Montana state line. Extensive excavations at the site by John Brumley in the mid-1970s indicate a long history of bison hunting, including at least ten cultural occupations documented in more than 19,000 square feet of excavations. Seven of the ten episodes of site use were by Middle Archaic hunter-gatherers. Dated to between 4,500 and 3,500 years ago, Cactus Flower's Middle Archaic components yielded a minimum of forty bison, probably procured in groups of three to five animals on several different occasions. In addition to bison (the staple of the diet), pronghorn were also hunted, along with a variety of small game, including deer, dog, fox, rabbit, shellfish, and birds.

Dozens of McKean projectile points were recovered at the site, including one produced from obsidian. The nearest sources of obsidian are to the south at Bear Gulch, Idaho, and Obsidian Cliff in Yellowstone National Park, Wyoming, suggesting travel to the south through Montana. Shell from a marine organism was also recovered, indicating trade connections to the west coast, and Knife River Flint was present, suggesting contact with groups in western North Dakota.

A circle of stones surrounding a central hearth dated at 5,000 to 4,500 years old was also identified in the McKean occupations. Brumley interpreted this as one of the earliest examples of a stone circle in the northern Great Plains. The presence of this well-dated stone circle supports the data collected at Airport Rings in Gardiner, suggesting that the use of shelters secured with stones was initiated during the Middle Archaic period.

LONG CREEK SITE

The Long Creek Site in southern Saskatchewan includes a detailed record of two Middle Archaic occupations dating to approximately 4,700 years ago. The site is located along a terrace of Long Creek, a tributary of the Souris River. In addition to Oxbow projectile points, a variety of stone and bone tools were recovered at the site. The two occupations contained four to five and eight to nine bison, respectively, while one of the occupations also contained three dog or coyote. Excavations also revealed the outline of a circular feature with interior post molds, suggesting use as a hide-tanning structure. Generally, the site was used to process bison.

LIGHTNING SPRING SITE

Excavated by James Keyser and colleagues, the Lightning Spring Site is located in a small spring-fed basin with stands of ponderosa pine in the North Cave Hills, a northern extension of the Black Hills in South Dakota. The Middle Archaic components contained fourteen McKean projectile points produced from Knife River Flint, porcellanite, and local materials. This stone suite indicates travel or trade to the north and west into Montana and North Dakota. Six radiocarbon dates from the site indicate multiple occupations between 4,200 and 3,430 years ago.

Animal remains were dominated by pronghorn (77 percent) and bison (16 percent). In 1995, Keyser and James Wettstaed suggested that even though pronghorn dominate in terms of bone count, bison would have provided more total meat (about 400 to 800 pounds) compared to pronghorn (about 50 pounds). The authors conclude that hunter-gatherers at Lightning Spring continued the Altithermal pattern of diverse subsistence. In one layer at the site, there were ten to thirteen bifaces produced from local stone, all of which are thought to be middle- to late-stage McKean point preforms. Each of the bifaces and McKean projectile points shows clear evidence of the use of heat treatment to facilitate the manufacture of stone tools.

BEAVER CREEK SHELTER

In Wind Cave National Park in the Black Hills of South Dakota, the Beaver Creek Shelter provides a record of transition from Early to Middle Archaic. In addition to its Early Archaic occupation, radiocarbon dates indicate multiple Middle Archaic occupations between 4,700 and 3,870 years ago. McKean projectile points were recovered in the Middle Archaic levels. James Martin and Lynn Alex of the Iowa state archaeologist office suggest continuity in site use between the Early and Middle Archaic occupations, based on similar stone tool and resource use. Bison, deer, and pronghorn remains were observed at the site, although it is unclear if these were all represented in the Middle Archaic site levels.

MCKEAN SITE

In 1954, William Mulloy was the first to excavate at the McKean Site, with additional work completed by the University of Wyoming in the 1980s and 1990s under the direction of Marcel Kornfeld. The McKean Site is located at the far western edge of the Black Hills near what is now the Keyhole Reservoir, produced by the damming of the Belle Fourche River. Excavations between 1983 and 1985 yielded over forty-three thousand artifacts from more than 84 cubic meters of excavations. Included among these artifacts were twenty-one McKean and twenty Middle Archaic Duncan/Hanna points, along with a variety of other stone tools. Kornfeld and his colleagues also analyzed a cache of seven McKean artifacts, including six scraping tools and a large flake. The tools were produced from a variety of stones. Dates for this site ranged from 4,590 to 3,287 years old.

More than thirteen thousand bone fragments were recovered at the site as well, but of the more than eight hundred identifiable bones, most were from recently deceased leopard frogs. Bison remains account for most of the identifiable prehistoric animal remains, with sixty-six total fragments, compared to forty-one deer, twenty-eight rabbit, twenty-five pronghorn, and a variety of small burrowing animals, probably intrusive into the site. There is no indication that bison hunting had yet gained center stage at the McKean Site.

LEIGH CAVE

Leigh Cave, located in a rock outcrop on the western slopes of the Bighorn Mountains, yielded a mat of plants, including wild onion bulbs, buffalo berry, prickly pear cactus, chokecherry, pine nuts, yucca, and wild rose hips, all of which were likely used by the Middle Archaic site occupants. Fragments of cord produced from milkweed, juniper bark, and grasses were found at the site as well. Wood shavings from chokecherry, cottonwood, willow, and western birch were found littered on the floor, suggesting woodworking. These plant, wood, and cordage remains were located near a fire hearth containing the remains of hundreds of crickets that were probably roasted for food. George Frison reports a radiocarbon date of 4,170 years at Leigh Cave. Along with Mummy Cave to the west, Leigh Cave provides outstanding insights into the diverse universe of plants and insects utilized by Middle Archaic hunter-gatherers in the greater Bighorn Basin of Wyoming and Montana.

MEDICINE LODGE CREEK SITE

Near Leigh Cave in the Bighorn Mountains, the Medicine Lodge Creek Site has yielded substantial Middle Archaic artifacts in addition to its Late Paleoindian ones. Radiocarbon dates place the Middle Archaic occupations at Medicine Lodge Creek between approximately 4,050 and 3,750 years ago. The main Middle Archaic occupation had several McKean-style points. One of the projectile points was found within a Middle Archaic activity area that contained two large nodules of phosphoria chert, indicating that the area was used in the manufacture of stone tools from local sources. Bone fragments from the Middle Archaic occupations indicate a diverse suite of subsistence activities, including the hunting of bison, bighorn sheep, deer, and a variety of small mammals. However, fewer animal remains were recovered in these levels than from the preceding Late Paleoindian and subsequent Late Archaic occupations.

DEAD INDIAN CREEK SITE

The Dead Indian Creek Site, radiocarbon dated to between 4,400 and 3,800 years ago, was a winter campsite in the Sunlight Basin of northwestern Wyoming. Along with several McKean projectile points, the remains of at least fifty mule deer and lesser numbers of bighorn sheep and pronghorn were recovered the site. Five of the deer antler racks were arranged within a shallow pit feature, in all likelihood indicating a ritual associated with the hunt. The site also features one of the few pit houses in the northern portion of Wyoming. Originally interpreted as a former stream channel, the feature has since been identified as a Middle Archaic pit house with storage pits in its interior, as well as a hearth.

FISHING BRIDGE POINT SITE

In the summer of 2009, a team from the University of Montana excavated the Fishing Bridge Point Site on the shore of Yellowstone Lake in Yellowstone National Park. Three hearths were dated to approximately 3,100 and 2,900 years ago. One contained a Middle Archaic McKean projectile point, while another yielded a large red ochre cobble likely used in the manufacture of pigment for painting. Wood in the hearths was identified as lodgepole pine, but few other plant remains were identified. Obsidian composed approximately 90 percent of the stone assemblage, while Crescent Hill chert from near Mammoth Hot Springs was present

Excavation at the Fishing Bridge Point Site on the shore of Yellowstone Lake in Yellowstone National Park in Wyoming

at the site as well. Ongoing research at this site is likely to provide additional information regarding life during the end of the Middle Archaic, approximately 3,000 years ago.

MUMMY CAVE

Mummy Cave, along the North Fork of the Shoshone River in northwestern Wyoming, epitomizes the archaeology of the Middle Archaic period in the Rocky Mountains and Great Plains of Montana and vicinity. An amazing array of cultural debris supports the contention that Mummy Cave was heavily occupied during the Middle Archaic period. The sheer

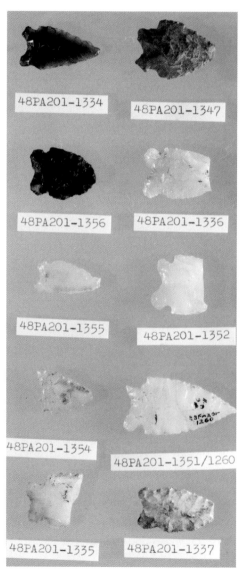

48PA201-1334

48PA201-1347

48PA201-1356

48PA201-1336

48PA201-1355

48PA201-1352

48PA201-1354

48PA201-1351/1260

48PA201-1335

48PA201-1337

McKean projectile points from Mummy Cave — Courtesy of Buffalo Bill Historical Center, Cody, Wyoming; gift of Harold McCracken, Mummy Cave Collection; Jack Richard photo; PN.29.48PA201-L21.

diversity of wild plants and animals found there, as well as bone, antler, wood, and fiber artifacts, shows that Middle Archaic hunter-gatherers exploited all available resources from a wide variety of habitats.

As reported in Wilfred Husted and Robert Edgar's 2002 report on Mummy Cave, radiocarbon dates from the Middle Archaic occupations—identified as cultural layer 30—range from 4,420 to 4,090 years ago. Two radiocarbon dates in cultural layer 28 also have Middle Archaic dates, probably indicating mixing downward from layer 30 into layer 28. Cultural layer 30 contained twenty-four fire pits, some measuring up to 3 feet in diameter. At least twenty-six McKean projectile points that lack side-notching were recovered, in addition to sixty-two McKean points with side-notching and deep basal indentation. A plethora of bifacial knives, stone scraping tools, drills, choppers, and other stone tools were also recovered in this layer.

The range of nonstone artifacts in culture layer 30 is astounding, including a wide variety of bone awls, pressure flakers for stone tool manufacture, scapula knives and tools, and tubular pipes, including one with a thick carbon cake from extensive use in smoking. Wooden tools

Rabbit bone beads and bead preforms from Pictograph Cave —Courtesy of Montana State Parks, a division of Montana Fish, Wildlife, and Parks

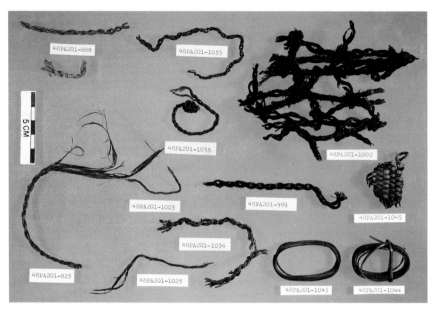

Textiles from Mummy Cave —Courtesy of Buffalo Bill Historical Center, Cody, Wyoming; gift of Harold McCracken, Mummy Cave Collection; Jack Richard photo; PN.29.48PA201-L17

were also abundant in the cave, including a tapered atlatl dart foreshaft, digging sticks for roots and tubers, and an assortment of pointed sticks.

Mummy Cave also yielded bone beads similar to those found in Pictograph Cave near Billings. Beads from both sites, as well as from the Spiro Site, were produced from the bones of rabbits and other small mammals. Long bones from the animals were cleaned and then cut with stone tools into bead sections. After separation, each section was polished and finished for use in jewelry.

In addition to the variety of bone and wood tools, a number of woven textiles were recovered from the Middle Archaic occupations at Mummy Cave. These include cordage produced from yucca, sagebrush bark, and juniper, probably used in the production of nets for hunting bighorn sheep. Coiled basketry produced from willow was found at the site as well. The wealth of artifacts from the Middle Archaic McKean site occupations suggests the immigration of Shoshone language speakers into the region at least as far back as this time and possibly earlier. A continuity of use at the cave into the Late Prehistoric period suggests the cave's occupants shared a similar culture.

Finally, as with all of the other occupation levels at Mummy Cave, bighorn sheep accounted for the most common animal, remains from the Middle Archaic cultural layer. Among other animals including duck, grouse, marmot, ground squirrel, beaver, porcupine, bear, and fox, cultural layer 30 revealed two deer and two bighorn sheep.

The Early Buffalo Hunters

The Late Plains Archaic Period

3,000 TO 1,500 YEARS AGO

During the Late Plains Archaic period, bison hunting emerged as the dominant subsistence pattern for people of the Great Plains east of the Continental Divide, while a diverse subsistence continued for those living west of the Divide. In both areas, side- and corner-notched projectile points were used in hunting. Great Plains bison hunting continued virtually unaltered (in basic form) until the introduction and mass adoption of the horse in the seventeenth and eighteenth centuries.

Archaeologists have traced cultural attributes from contemporary tribes to specific archaeological sites from the Late Archaic period. Based on the continuity of use, Head-Smashed-In in Alberta can almost certainly be attributed to the Blackfeet, and Mummy Cave in Wyoming to the Shoshone. These sites, thus, mark the presence of these tribes in their traditional cultural territories. Unfortunately, prior to the Late Archaic, gaps in use occur at these sites that prevent us from directly linking them to any specific ethnic or tribal group. They may have been there, and almost certainly were, but it is difficult to link sites to specific ethnic groups prior to the Late Archaic, or approximately 3,000 years ago.

During the Late Archaic, hunter-gatherers of Montana increased the distance they traveled, probably due to wide-ranging bison herds and the need to find them. This increased travel was facilitated by the use of the dog travois, a simple device dragged behind a dog to carry gear. Sites including Spring Creek Cave and Mummy Cave in Wyoming contain wooden artifacts that probably are the remains of travois. The overall population in Montana may have also increased during this period, as reflected by the substantially higher numbers of sites dating to the Late Archaic than to the preceding Middle and Early Archaic periods. However, as proposed by Tom Foor of the University of Montana in 1982, it is likely that heightened mobility simply translated into additional living sites, or camps. Also, more recent sites may have survived to be found because there has been less time for them to erode away or be buried by sediment.

Another reason for the higher number of sites in the Late Archaic is the relatively easy identification of the stone circles used to secure shelters.

Late Archaic projectile points from Pictograph Cave —Courtesy of Montana State Parks, a division of Montana Fish, Wildlife, and Parks

Crow woman and children with a horse and travois in 1883. Dogs were used to pull travois before horses were introduced to Montana in the eighteenth century.
—Courtesy of Archives and Special Collections, Mansfield Library, University of Montana

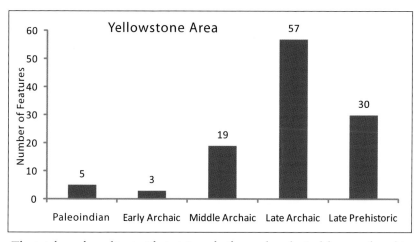

The total number of projectile points and other archaeological features found in Yellowstone National Park is much higher from the Late Archaic period than from other periods. —Data from fieldwork by teams from the University of Montana, 2007–2009

To facilitate the high mobility of bison hunting, hunter-gatherers increased their use of portable hide structures, or tepees. Thousands of stone circles marking the former locations of lodges can be found in Montana. Stone circles were used with increasing frequency during the Late Archaic and the subsequent Late Prehistoric.

This increase in sites, which is reflected all across the region, is confirmed by the University of Montana's surveys of Yellowstone National Park. During three seasons of archaeological survey of more than 4,000 acres, archaeologists identified fifty-seven Late Archaic features and points, compared to a combined twenty-two projectile points from the Early and Middle Archaic. Not only did the site count increase, the number of artifacts at each site increased, suggesting either rising populations or better preservation.

While the Late Archaic period witnessed extensive use of buffalo jumps, dog travois, tepees, and other innovations of highly mobile hunter-gatherers, I should also note that one important "last" occurred as well: the innovation of the bow and arrow approximately 1,500 years ago spelled the end of the atlatl, the hunting weapon of choice during the Late Archaic. Few dart points are recovered at sites dating after that time.

Bison Hunting

Hunting in the Great Plains, Rockies, and Columbia Plateau during the Late Archaic was not a subtle enterprise. As described so well in Jack Brink's *Imagining Head-Smashed-In* (2008) and in George C. Frison's

Survival by Hunting (2004), hunters actively engaged in complex, cooperative endeavors focused on the procurement of game, including bison, deer, pronghorn, and bighorn sheep.

While introduced and used sporadically during preceding time periods, bison jumps and corrals were used all over the northwestern Great Plains and Rocky Mountains with increased intensity beginning 3,000 years ago. Bison jumps required a complex arrangement of features, including bison aggregation areas with water, open areas conducive to driving bison, and the cliff itself. Hunters altered their environment to facilitate the hunt, building drive lines—composed of hundreds of large rocks organized into parallel or converging lines or avenues—for dozens of miles from the jump, and occasionally built corrals to trap the animals once driven over the precipice.

People actively participated in the bison drives, pushing the animals along the drive lines using brightly colored flags, brush piles, and fire to keep them moving forward to the kill location. Montana was the center of the bison jumping universe, with hundreds of such locations spread across the state east of the Rocky Mountains.

Trade

Bison was a commodity across the Great Plains, and nomadic hunters traded bison meat, hides, and tools with neighboring groups who were unable to regularly hunt bison. In particular, Knife River Flint from North Dakota and obsidian from Yellowstone National Park have been found at Late Archaic midwestern Woodland-period archaeological sites—especially those of the Hopewell Culture—in Ohio, Pennsylvania, and Michigan, among other states.

Most of these goods are thought to have been transported via trade along the major river systems that connect the Rocky Mountains and Great Plains with the eastern United States. For example, it is easy to imagine obsidian being traded down the Yellowstone River to the Missouri River then subsequently into the Mississippi River valley and points east. However, Warren DeBoer has proposed that some individuals within the Scioto River Hopewell Culture of Ohio may have traveled to Montana and Wyoming to obtain rare goods for use in ceremonies. Such goods include obsidian, Knife River Flint, and bison products, as well as bighorn sheep horns. University of Montana researchers found a large obsidian point in Yellowstone National Park that resembles Hopewell artifacts.

In association with this trade, Late Archaic hunter-gatherers actively sought out new sources of raw material and intensively mined them for stone. Numerous chert quarries in Montana—including the Schmitt Chert Quarry near Three Forks, the South Everson Creek Quarry near Dillon, and the Knife River Flint Quarries in western North Dakota—were mined

This large projectile point, found near Yellowstone Lake in Wyoming, was produced from Obsidian Cliff obsidian and resembles Hopewell artifacts.

for chert to be traded across the region. The hunter-gatherers also needed raw material to replace projectiles worn out by the intensive hunting of bison. Large pits were excavated, confirming that these Late Archaic people were the original Montana hard-rock miners.

Pelican Lake and Besant Projectile Points

The most diagnostic artifacts from the Late Archaic are Pelican Lake and Besant projectile points. The corner-notched Pelican Lake points were utilized during the entire Late Archaic period—from 3,000 to 1,500 years ago—with some researchers suggesting an even earlier adoption at approximately 3,500 years ago. The side-notched Besant projectile points were used from approximately 2,000 to 1,300 years ago, thus extending into the Late Prehistoric period.

Pelican Lake projectile points are deeply corner-notched—creating sharp barbs on the corners—with straight blades and straight bases. The blade is triangular and the finely made notches are narrow, elongated, and U-shaped. Pelican Lake projectile points were well manufactured, especially compared to their later Besant counterparts. Blades on some Pelican Lake points are serrated, but most are not. Pelican Lake points range from 20 to 50 millimeters long, 15 to 35 millimeters wide, and 3 to 8 millimeters thick.

Pelican Lake projectile point (left) and Besant projectile point (right). The following traits help distinguish Besant and Pelican Lake projectile points: Besant projectile points are not as finely manufactured as Pelican Lake points; Besant points have slightly convex blades versus straight blades for Pelican Lake; Besant points have side notches versus Pelican Lake's sharply barbed corner notches; and Besant point bases vary in shape more than Pelican Lake points, which more typically have straight bases.

Besant projectile points have triangular to lanceolate blades with straight to convex blade shapes. Their maximum width is at the shoulder, with simply produced, U-shaped side notches. The point base is concave to straight but occasionally convex. As defined by Charles Zeier in 1983 from studying an assemblage of some 280 Besant projectile points from the Antonsen Site near Bozeman, typical Besant points measure 20 to 75 millimeters long (mean 25–40 mm), 9 to 26 millimeters wide (mean 16–20 mm), and 2.6 to 9.0 millimeters thick (mean 4.3–6.0 mm). Zeier characterized the Besant point as the "last atlatl dart point." Approximately 1,500 years ago, hunter-gatherers quickly adopted bow and arrow technology, resulting in the demise of Late Archaic Pelican Lake and Besant points.

While not common, some Late Archaic sites have yielded both Besant and Pelican Lake points from the same cultural deposits. For example, two Pelican Lake points and one Besant point were found in the same strata at Medicine Lodge Creek in Wyoming, with all of them dating to approximately 1,560 years ago. However, it is far more common to have one type or the other within a specific cultural deposit.

Pictograph Cave in Billings and Spring Creek Cave in the Bighorn Mountains of Wyoming have yielded projectile points still hafted to wooden shafts. These finds have allowed archaeologists to interpret *all* Archaic notched projectile points as likely atlatl dart points (as opposed to spear or arrow tips). The wooden shafts have not been found in sites from earlier times, probably because they are subject to rotting.

Side-notched projectile point from Pictograph Cave hafted to a foreshaft with cordage and pine pitch mixed with charcoal. —Courtesy of Montana State Parks, a division of Montana Fish, Wildlife, and Parks

Besant Pottery

Another important technological innovation of Late Archaic tribes was the first—albeit limited—use of pottery. Besant pottery is rare in Montana but is found on occasion dating to between 2,000 and 1,500 years ago in sites in the northern tier of the state, especially in the northeastern corner. Besant pottery in Montana likely was derived via trade and cultural contact with emerging village groups in the Missouri River valley to the south and east. Besant pottery is of comparatively low quality and was generally globular-shaped via coiling. It was constructed by placing linear segments of clay atop one another into a pot shape. Exterior designs on Besant pottery were plain or simple cord markings. Grit was used as a temper to strengthen the clay and reduce the chances of pot breakage during firing and use.

Besant pottery vessels were probably used on occasion to facilitate cooking and storage but may also have been special ceremonial items. However, it is uncommon for any highly mobile group to use lots of pottery due to its bulky nature. Most hunter-gatherers used baskets or leather pouches for transport of goods.

Late Plains Archaic Sites in Montana

So many Late Archaic archaeological sites have been identified and excavated in Montana and the surrounding region that it is impossible to discuss them all here. I focus on a handful of the best examples of Late Archaic

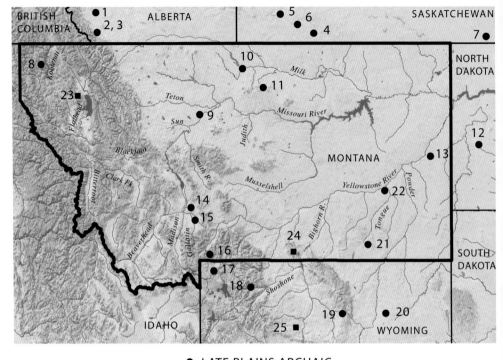

● LATE PLAINS ARCHAIC

1. Old Woman's
2. Kenney
3. Head-Smashed-In
4. Bracken Cairn
5. Sjovold
6. Mortlach
7. Long Creek
8. 24LN691
9. Carter Ferry

10. Wahkpa Chu'gn
11. Keaster
12. Knife River Flint Quarries
13. Mini-Moon
14. Schmitt Quarry
15. Antonsen
16. Yellowstone Bank Cache
17. Obsidian Cliff
18. Mummy Cave

19. Spring Creek Cave
20. Ruby Bison Pound
21. Kobold
22. Powers-Yonkee

■ ROCK ART
23. Kila Pictographs
24. Petroglyph Canyon
25. Legend Rock

Late Archaic Sites in Montana and the surrounding region

sites in the area. Generally, if both Pelican Lake and Besant complexes are present at the individual sites, I will discuss the Pelican Lake first.

SITE 24LN691

In northwestern Montana archaeological sites are abundant, reflecting long-term use of the Kootenai, Flathead, and Clark Fork valleys by hunter-gatherers. As of the mid-1990s, Becky Timmons at Kootenai National Forest and her fellow archaeologists had identified more than four hundred sites around the perimeter of Lake Koocanusa near Libby. Alston Thoms of Texas A&M University and formerly of the Center for Northwest Anthropology at Washington State University conducted test excavations at a number of these sites to evaluate whether they were eligible for listing on the National Register of Historic Places. One of the sites—24LN691—yielded a Late Archaic cooking feature along the Kootenai Flats area of northern Lake Koocanusa. The site is located among dune fields in sandy terrain near the Kootenai River inlet.

Thoms's team identified medium and large mammal bone fragments—probably deer and elk—from a rock-lined feature used to cook meat at the site. The charcoal in the feature was radiocarbon dated to approximately 1,980 years ago. A stone circle was identified nearby. Conical skin structures, sometimes with rocks used as weights around the base, were used by the Kootenai for shelter during the 1800s; the recovery of the stone circle at 24LN691 suggests their use far back into the Late Archaic period, at least 2,000 years ago.

The Yaak River near Libby was a popular camping area and travel corridor in the Late Archaic period.

COLUMBIA PLATEAU ROCK ART TRADITION

The Columbia Plateau Tradition, a rock art style dating to the Late Plains Archaic period, is found from western Montana west into the heart of the Columbia River region in Idaho, Washington, Oregon, and British Columbia. Much of the art depicts real-life events, such as hunting scenes with animals and people. One image from the Bitterroot valley of western Montana shows an individual holding an atlatl.

Columbia Plateau rock art at the Kila Pictographs west of Kalispell

104

Two of the more famous Columbia Plateau rock art sites are Buffalo Eddy near Lewiston, Idaho, and the Kila Pictographs west of Kalispell, Montana. At Buffalo Eddy, animals are depicted in association with humans holding weapons. Similar scenes are depicted at the Kila Pictographs, but instead of being pecked into the rock face as at Buffalo Eddy, the art was painted onto the rock using red pigment. Three extensive panels, protected with fencing, are present for public viewing along the north side of State Highway 2 west of Kalispell. These panels show a variety of animals and humans, several of which are in the Columbia Plateau Tradition and very similar to the triangle-bodied figures with horned headdresses at Buffalo Eddy and other rock art sites in the interior Northwest. Other rock art images at the site include bison and a wolf or coyote, all of which are rare in Montana rock art. Carling Malouf of the University of Montana spent a good deal of his career identifying and recording rock art of the Columbia Plateau Tradition in the Bitterroot and Flathead regions of Montana.

WAHKPA CHU'GN BUFFALO JUMP

The Wahkpa Chu'gn Buffalo Jump is one of the most important buffalo jumps in the state of Montana, not only because of the outstanding archaeology conducted there but also because the site features one of the best on-site archaeological museums anywhere in the northern Great Plains. Located behind a mall in Havre, Wahkpa Chu'gn is easily accessible to tourists and contains intact excavations that can be viewed by visitors. Wahkpa Chu'gn was first identified at the base of a bluff overlooking the Milk River in 1962 by archaeologist John Brumley, who is now the caretaker for the site. The Montana Archaeological Society excavated the site in the 1960s and 1970s with the help of the H. Earl Clack Museum in Havre. Along with Brumley, Leslie Davis of Montana State University was one of the key archaeologists to work at the site. Above the cliff is a broad and flat landform suitable to gathering bison herds and then running them via drives toward the cliff. Below the cliff the Milk River, a perennial water source, facilitated animal processing.

Wahkpa Chu'gn has yielded at least six radiocarbon dates in the Besant cultural layers, ranging from 2,050 to 1,450 years ago, indicating the Besant people repeatedly used the site to kill bison. The Besant occupations have yielded hundreds of Besant projectile points in association

The Wahkpa Chu'gn Buffalo Jump (at left) and visitor center above the Milk River near Havre

with literally millions of bison bones from hundreds of individual animals. While a pound, or corral, was identified at the site, it likely dates to later occupations. There is no evidence of a pound used during the Late Archaic.

KOBOLD SITE

While first occupied during the Middle Archaic period, the Kobold Site contains an extensive series of Late Archaic bison kills as well. This site is located along Rosebud Creek, a small tributary of the Tongue River near Decker in southeastern Montana. As with Wahkpa Chu'gn, the Kobold Site is perfectly situated as a bison jump. Above the site, numerous springs and a wide gathering area are present, with ample space for bison drive lines. As many as eighty-six stone piles extend approximately 1,800 feet along the mesa top above the cliff, forming a V that converges toward the cliff edge. The sandstone escarpment over which the bison were driven measures approximately 25 feet tall and has a rock shelter in an overhang just below the cliff edge. Nearby Rosebud Creek provided a source of water for hunter-gatherers moving through the area.

Excavated in the late 1960s by the University of Wyoming under the direction of George Frison, the Late Archaic site occupations contained thirty-two intact projectile points, several of which resemble Pelican Lake and Besant styles. The site appears to have been utilized repeatedly

106

during the Late Archaic by people using both types of projectile points. An extensive number of butchering tools indicates that the Late Archaic occupations were intensive; however, only a small number of bones were recovered. Frison suggests that his research simply did not uncover the Late Archaic bone bed. He also suggests that if it had, the bed would have been substantially larger than the preceding Middle Archaic kill that yielded more than sixty animals.

MINI-MOON SITE

The Mini-Moon Site, another eastern Montana bison kill site, is located in the badlands of Dawson County near Glendive. The Yellowstone River flows approximately 3 miles to the west of the site. As reported by Susan Hughes in 1991, excavations at the Mini-Moon Site yielded two Late Archaic occupations dated to 1,920 and 1,520 years ago. The site was probably a short-term, warm-season camp used by mobile hunter-gatherers. While bison was the focus of their hunting, the site occupants also ate deer and other small mammals.

Bone marrow and grease had been extracted from bones, suggesting the preparation of pemmican. For Great Plains bison hunters, this activity was often completed during the fall in preparation for winter. A warm-season occupation is further indicated by the presence of sego lily, onion, and chenopodium—all plants available in summer and fall. Hughes suggested a sexual division of labor at the site, with men completing the initial bison hunting and processing and women completing the final animal preparation in a main base camp.

KEASTER SITE

Another important bison kill is the Keaster Site located northeast of Great Falls along the Missouri River Breaks. At an elevation of approximately 3,120 feet, the site overlooks the Missouri River within what is now the Upper Missouri River Breaks National Monument. The site was excavated between 1962 and 1964 under the leadership of Leslie Davis and Emmett Stallcop. Pelican Lake and Besant points were recovered from the Late Archaic component of this site, which extends for more than 250 feet along the riverbank. Animals were run over the Missouri River terrace edge down the escarpment and into a pound or trap constructed of wood. Yielding a date of approximately 1,950 years ago, the Keaster Site may be the earliest evidence of a bison pound in Montana, according to Tom Foor of the University of Montana.

CARTER FERRY BUFFALO JUMP

The Carter Ferry Buffalo Jump, located in Choteau County about three-quarters of a mile upstream along the Missouri River from the Carter

FOOTHILLS ABSTRACT ROCK ART TRADITION

The Foothills Abstract Tradition of rock art shows spiritual images as pictographs at sites in central Montana dating to the last 2,000 years. The esoteric nature of the images helps distinguish them from Columbia Plateau rock art, which most commonly shows humans and animals. The Foothills Abstract Tradition is found at several rock shelters and caves within the Sweetgrass Hills, Little Rocky Mountains, and Little Belt Mountains, as well as along the Smith, Yellowstone, Bighorn, Musselshell, and Missouri river valleys. The images were produced using red ochre and include bears, handprints, smeared walls, and animals connected to humans with lines. Some of the humans have elongated bodies, arms, and legs, likely suggesting a spiritual event. Other images depict geometric shapes incorporating human elements and probably also reflect some sort of vision quest or spiritually meaningful event. The most common image in the Foothills Abstract Tradition is a bear shown in profile, often in association with human handprints. For this reason, some archaeologists interpret the images to be representative of a bear cult among the people who produced the art during the Late Archaic and into the Late Prehistoric. True or not, the association of bears with human hands indicates the importance of bears in the spiritual lives of local hunter-gatherers at that time. For contemporary tribes, bears are powerful beings that can make warriors strong, and make spiritual leaders wise. Being able to harness the power of the bear was probably important on multiple levels for hunter-gatherers of central Montana.

Foothills Abstract rock art at Site 24LC1147 north of Helena —Mavis and John Greer photo

Ferry boat landing, also yielded Pelican Lake projectile points. They were found 18 feet below the cliff top. Maynard Shumate of Montana State University infers use of a bison pound at this site.

ANTONSEN SITE

The Antonsen Site, a buffalo kill site, was first recorded by Carling Malouf and subsequently excavated by a team from Montana State University in the early 1970s under the direction of Leslie Davis and Charles Zeier. At an elevation of approximately 4,850 feet, the Antonsen Site is located within the southern Gallatin River valley approximately 6 miles west of Bozeman. While not a bison jump per se, the site is directly below a river terrace escarpment with a vertical drop of approximately 12 to 15 feet.

Late Archaic hunter-gatherers drove bison along the upper river terrace over the escarpment to the lower terrace, where they killed the animals using atlatls tipped with Besant and Pelican Lake darts. Davis and Zeier report two occupations, including a large Besant occupation about 1,600 years ago and a smaller Pelican Lake occupation about 1,750 years ago. At least two hundred bison are estimated to have been killed in two main areas during the Besant occupations.

Various cherts and basalts from southwestern Montana sources account for the majority of stone material found with the Besant occupations. As would be expected of regional Late Archaic sites, a few projectile points

The Gallatin River valley with river terraces like those at the Antonsen Site near Bozeman

109

were fashioned from Knife River Flint and obsidian. In 1983, Zeier conducted an analysis of 280 Besant projectile points from the Antonsen Site, resulting in an excellent understanding of how they were produced.

SCHMITT QUARRY

The Schmitt Quarry is located in uplands north of Three Forks, in an area of abundant natural resources, not least of which is a large exposure of Madison Formation limestone that contains a large vein of highly desirable dark bluish gray chert. As reported by Leslie Davis of Montana State University in 1982, twelve radiocarbon dates on wood charcoal from the quarry complex indicate its extensive use between approximately 3,400 and 1,600 years ago. The quarry workshop measures more than 200 acres and includes numerous stone-reduction camps, as well as four stone circles and the open-pit mine.

Leslie Davis giving a tour of the Schmitt Quarry near Three Forks

YELLOWSTONE BANK CACHE

The Yellowstone Bank Cache is a campsite along the Yellowstone River just north of Gardiner in the northernmost portion of Yellowstone National Park. The Yellowstone Bank Cache is one of fourteen archaeological sites that my team from the University of Montana excavated within the Gardiner Basin in 2007. Four roasting pit features indicate the presence of multiple occupations during the latter portion of the Late Archaic period, one between 2,500 and 2,200 years ago, and another approximately 1,600 years ago. This period of occupation is supported by four radiocarbon dates and the presence of three Pelican Lake corner-notched projectile points. This site functioned as a seasonal camp through which Late Archaic hunter-gatherers traveled from the Yellowstone Plateau to the northern Great Plains.

Each of the hearths was densely packed with fire-cracked rock and local vegetation. Sagebrush, juniper, pine, alder, and maple were used as fuel in the hearths. Food processing activities are indicated by the presence of heavily processed medium- and large-sized animals, including deer and several other indeterminate species, and plant debris including chenopodium seeds and pinecones. Similar animal and plant remains were recovered from the nearby Late Archaic Site 24YE14, including deer and chenopodium.

The site was used intensively for toolmaking, with hunter-gatherers producing knives of obsidian and Crescent Hill chert. Other tools were made as well, including unifaces, sidescrapers, and an endscraper. The Obsidian Cliff obsidian and Crescent Hill chert come from sources approximately 20 miles east and south of the Yellowstone Bank Cache, respectively. The Obsidian Cliff source would have been accessed by following the Yellowstone River upstream to the Gardner River and then to Obsidian Creek—the route taken by U.S. 89 through Yellowstone

A Late Archaic hearth at the Yellowstone Bank Cache near Gardiner

National Park today. The trip required an increase in elevation of some 2,200 feet from the valley floor to the top of the Yellowstone Plateau, at about 7,500 feet. To reach Crescent Hill chert, people had a slightly easier route, following the Yellowstone River upstream for approximately 20 miles through the Black Canyon of the Yellowstone, then traversing feeder streams into the uplands to the Crescent Hill basalt formation from which the chert derives. The trip to the Crescent Hill chert source required a climb of between 1,300 to 2,300 feet, depending on which of several chert outcrops was used.

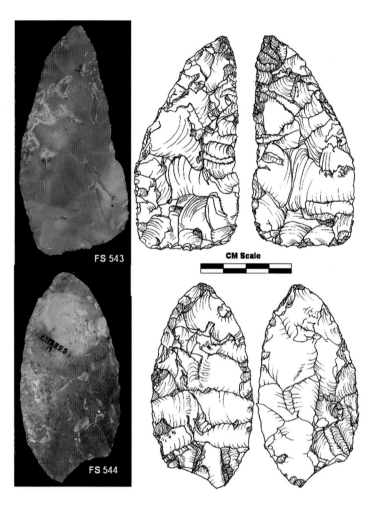

FS 543

CM Scale

FS 544

Two bifaces made of chert from the Yellowstone Bank Cache near Gardiner —Meg Tracy illustration

112

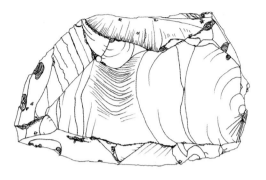

*Large obsidian
biface from RJP-1
Site in Yellowstone
National Park.
Biface measures 16.4
centimeters in length.*
—Meg Tracy illustration

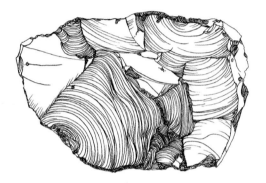

Late Plains Archaic Sites outside Montana

HEAD-SMASHED-IN BUFFALO JUMP

The Head-Smashed-In Buffalo Jump is one of the most important bison jumps in the world and is listed as an UNESCO World Heritage Site. The name of the site derives from a Native American story regarding the demise of a young boy who got caught up in the buffalo jump. Historic Blackfeet narratives and consistent use of the site link Head-Smashed-In to the Blackfeet Culture, at least as far back as the Late Archaic occupations. The site has been used as a buffalo jump for at least 6,000 years. While use in the Early Archaic period was brief, the intensity of site use escalated beginning 3,000 years ago, with numerous occupations during the Late Archaic and Late Prehistoric periods.

The site is located approximately 60 miles north of the Montana state line, west of Lethbridge, Alberta, in the Porcupine Hills approximately a half mile north of the Oldman River. As described in Jack Brink's 2008 book on the site, it is one of the best examples of a bison hunting complex anywhere in the Great Plains. The most significant landform is the cliff, which is a 1,000-foot-long escarpment standing approximately 30 feet tall. Above the cliff is a wide-open gathering basin that includes several

View north toward the cliff at Head-Smashed-In Buffalo Jump, Alberta, Canada

streams and multiple drive lines stretching for miles to the north. More than five hundred stone piles have been identified above the jump, marking the avenues through which bison were run over the cliff. The Oldman River below the site provides ample flat terraces and access to fresh water for the large numbers of bison hunters and their families who gathered here, especially in the fall during preparation for winter.

Brian Reeves led excavations at the site during the late 1960s and 1970s, with additional work done in the 1980s prior to and during construction of the World Heritage Site museum. Much of the excavation occurred just below the cliff in the bison-processing areas, but additional excavations occurred at the campsite, located a few hundred feet to the south below the jump.

In the southern portion of the bison-processing area, excavations identified three major Pelican Lake occupations, as well as smaller portions of a Besant occupation. One mixed Pelican Lake/Besant occupation was radiocarbon dated to approximately 1,975 years ago and was buried nearly 2 feet below the ground surface. In the northern portion of the processing area, a mixed Pelican Lake/Besant occupation was dated to between 1,550 and 1,400 years ago. Below this, five additional Pelican Lake site occupations were excavated down to a depth of 25 feet below the ground surface. The earliest radiocarbon-dated Pelican Lake occupation at the site occurred between 3,100 and 2,750 years ago.

These occupations yielded an unknown number of bison, but likely included hundreds, if not thousands, of animals. While most of the bison were butchered using stone tools made from local materials, evidence of long-distance trade is present in the form of obsidian from Yellowstone National Park and Knife River Flint from North Dakota. While Besant projectile points are limited at the site, they do seem to occur with Pelican Lake points, perhaps suggesting that single cultural groups employed both projectile forms, or that people from different cultural groups used the site either together or at closely spaced intervals during the Late Archaic.

KENNEY SITE

The Kenney Site, a Late Archaic camp on a terrace of the Oldman River to the west of Head-Smashed-In, yielded evidence of two major Late Archaic Besant occupations dating to between 1,650 and 1,500 years ago. As would be expected in this valley, bison hunting was the main subsistence focus of Besant peoples. In the initial Besant occupation, thirteen bison were taken at the site, as was a single deer, while in the later Besant occupation, seven bison were taken, along with a pronghorn. Brian Reeves recovered fifty-nine Besant projectile points at the site, which was a secondary bison butchering and stone retooling location. Such secondary camps are typically located in association with large kill sites such as Head-Smashed-In. Many of them—including several along the Oldman River—also have stone circles, indicating use of tepees as shelter during bison hunting in the area.

OLD WOMAN'S BUFFALO JUMP

Old Woman's Buffalo Jump, another important bison kill site in the northern Great Plains, is famous as the place where the Old Woman's point, a small, Late Prehistoric type of arrow point, was first found and described. However, the earliest occupations at the jump occurred during the Late Archaic period. The buffalo jump is located about 50 miles to the north of Head-Smashed-In on a tributary stream of the Oldman River near Cayley, Alberta. The setting is similar to that at Head-Smashed-In and includes a large upland gathering basin above a 15- to 20-foot-tall cliff. Richard Forbis identified twenty-nine different cultural layers in his excavations at the site during the 1950s and 1960s. The major Late Archaic occupations contained dozens of bison, along with Besant projectile points, in a cultural layer dated to between 1,900 and 1,600 years ago.

The name Old Woman's Buffalo Jump stems from a traditional Blackfeet narrative describing how men and women cooperate toward the success of the hunt and in life at large. Much cooperation between men and women, young and old, had to occur at Old Woman's Buffalo Jump, where bison bones cover the ground beneath the cliff to a depth of several feet.

LATE ARCHAIC SITES IN SASKATCHEWAN

Numerous other Late Archaic sites are present across the Great Plains and northern Rocky Mountains in the Canadian provinces, including several within Saskatchewan worthy of discussion. Among these is the Mortlach Site near Pelican Lake, where in 1955 Boyd Wettlaufer was the first to describe the distinctive Late Archaic Pelican Lake projectile point. He identified at least four Pelican Lake site occupations, along with others that were mixed with Besant points. The Long Creek Site yielded intensive Pelican Lake occupations. There, Pelican Lake points were found in levels dating to between 3,700 and 2,300 years ago, making it one of the earliest Pelican Lake sites in the region. The Sjovold Site yielded Pelican Lake points dating older than 3,200 years ago, perhaps indicating that the complex originated in this region and subsequently moved southward into Montana after 3,000 years ago.

The Bracken Cairn Site in Saskatchewan, described by Barbara Neal, contains a Late Archaic Pelican Lake human burial. This site yielded the remains of five individuals: an adult male, an adult female, two juveniles, and an individual of unknown age and sex. A Pelican Lake projectile point was found in the burial, along with beads, pendants, and other ceremonial items dated to 2,470 years ago.

KNIFE RIVER FLINT QUARRIES

Located in western North Dakota near Killdeer, the Knife River Flint Quarries are extensive, a mining operation on par with that at the Schmitt Quarry in Montana and the Obsidian Cliff quarry in Wyoming. The quarry complex covers hundreds of square miles and includes dozens of archaeological sites, including a large one on the property of the Lynch family. Matthew Root and Stanley Ahler both documented extensive quarrying at several sites in western North Dakota, while Michael Metcalf and Ahler similarly documented Late Archaic quarrying at the Alkali Creek Site in Dunn County, North Dakota. These quarries are located approximately 60 miles east of the Montana state line. Most sites in far eastern Montana contain a high percentage of Knife River Flint in their stone assemblages, particularly sites dating to the Late Archaic period.

Knife River Flint is a brown chalcedony that formed when peat was silicified. It is occasionally pure white due to the accumulation of varnish or patination upon exposure to sunlight. Most commonly, though, Knife River Flint is distinctively root beer brown and shows diagnostic ultraviolet light responses that allow it to be easily distinguished from other brown chalcedonies found throughout the region (for example, Bowman chert from northwestern Montana and South Everson Creek chert from southwestern Montana).

During the Late Archaic, miners excavated thousands of tons of gravels, leaving behind large open pits. Matthew Root noted that a single quarry pit at Site 32DU184 measured 3,000 square feet and was nearly 6 feet deep, likely created by hauling dirt, cobbles, and gravel out with baskets and discarding them on the mine rim and in a creek valley below. As described by Metcalf and Ahler in 1995, "The Late Archaic quarrying

Knife River Flint Quarries, Dunn County, North Dakota

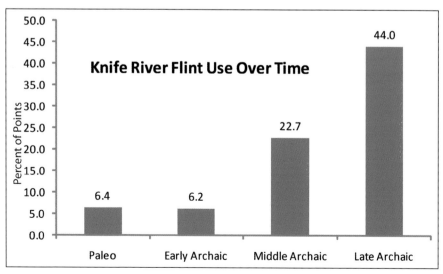

The use of Knife River Flint increased dramatically, from 6 percent of all points in the Paleoindian period to 44 percent of all points in the Late Archaic. —Data from Ahler, 1986

episode(s) included the excavation of numerous shaft type quarry pits which mushroom once the shaft penetrates the flint-bearing Knife River gravels. . . . Once the gravels were reached, they would have been excavated in a very limited and cramped space, essentially in the dark, and all selected materials removed to the surface."

RUBY BISON POUND SITE

One of the more interesting bison kill sites in the region is the Ruby Bison Pound Site in the Powder River basin of north-central Wyoming. George Frison interprets this bison kill site to be the remains of an impoundment by Besant hunters who had moved into the region from somewhere to the north after 1,700 years ago. In Wyoming, hunter-gatherers utilized pounds in lieu of adequate cliff-jumping landforms. Besant hunters constructed a complex corral of wood in order to collect bison as they were funneled downslope along the edge of a stream terrace. The structure probably resembled modern ranching corrals, suggesting an elaborate knowledge of bison behavior by Besant peoples. The Ruby Bison Pound measured about 40 feet in diameter and had more than twenty-five enclosing posts, with additional posts along the drive line where it entered the pound. Individuals probably lined up along the drive line to steer bison into the structure. Besant projectile points were concentrated in the gathering pound, and a few were found along the drive line as well. The Ruby bison pound structure could contain approximately twenty animals and was used during multiple annual or seasonal events in the fall in preparation for the coming winter. Frison estimates that it would have taken approximately twenty men about ten days to construct the elaborate wood corral, dated to between 1,800 and 1,500 years ago.

Downslope from the pound, Frison excavated a 10- to 15-inch-deep bison bone bed and a bison-processing area that measured approximately 10,000 square feet. A possibly religious structure measuring approximately 15 by 40 feet, with bison vertebrae placed in the post holes, suggests ritual preparation of the drive line and pound.

MUDDY CREEK SITE

The Muddy Creek Site, located approximately 90 miles south of the Ruby Bison Pound, is another bison pound, this one along the Little Medicine Bow River in south-central Wyoming. Here, as at the Ruby Bison Pound Site, Late Archaic hunter-gatherers constructed a wooden corral on a side slope. It measured approximately 40 feet wide and was placed in a well-hidden depression to hide the operation from bison that gathered in a flat area above the site. George Frison estimates that the Muddy Creek bison pound could contain a herd of about twenty bison and indicates that it was used during multiple kill episodes.

MUMMY CAVE

Mummy Cave, an upland site along the Shoshone River east of Yellowstone National Park in Wyoming, had significant early occupations and continued to be used through the Late Archaic and into the Late Prehistoric. As reported by Wilfred Husted and Robert Edgar, the Late Archaic occupations at Mummy Cave date to between 2,800 and 2,000 years ago and are near the ground surface of the cave in cultural layers 32 and 34. Bighorn sheep dominate the animal remains found in these layers, which also include a variety of small mammal remains.

Cultural layer 32 yielded eleven Pelican Lake projectile points within a component dating to approximately 2,800 years ago. It also contained an assortment of knives and scraping tools, as well as two bone pressure flakers and two cordage fragments measuring 2 to 4 inches long.

Cultural layer 34 from Mummy Cave yielded seventeen Late Archaic projectile points—including both Pelican Lake and Besant varieties—dating to approximately 2,000 years ago. Three rock-filled roasting pits were identified in this layer, all of which measured approximately 2 feet

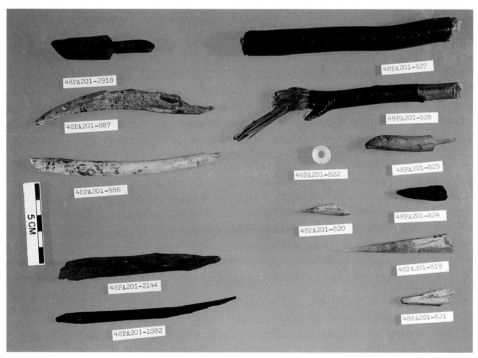

Late Archaic bone, shell, and wood items from Mummy Cave, Wyoming
—Courtesy of Buffalo Bill Historical Center, Cody, Wyoming; gift of Harold McCracken, Mummy Cave Collection; Jack Richard photo; PN.29.48PA201-L15

DINWOODY ROCK ART TRADITION

The Dinwoody Tradition is an important regional Late Archaic rock art tradition of northwestern Wyoming and south-central Montana. Etched into cliff faces within the last 2,000 years, these petroglyphs are among the most unusual in North America. Humanlike figures connect to animallike figures with zigzag lines and other geometric symbols. Some of the images are so strange that they are likely the result of hallucinations, vision quest events by coming-of-age individuals, or other religious activities. Sites like Legend Rock near Thermopolis, Wyoming, are the heartland of

the Dinwoody Tradition, but Petroglyph Canyon in Bighorn Canyon in southcentral Montana also has some Dinwoody images. Radiocarbon and cationratio dating of Dinwoody art at Legend Rock places its initial appearance at approximately 2,000 years ago and indicates that it continued for about 1,000 years.

Dinwoody rock art at Legend Rock near Thermopolis, Wyoming

in diameter. Bone tools in layer 34 include awls and pressure flakers, while a shell bead was also recovered. Two long, cylindrical, wooden projectile shafts were also found. One was intended for use with a stone inset, while the other was for use with a socketed foreshaft and projectile. The terminal end of a third wooden foreshaft was also recovered; this item was pointed on the distal (haft) end with numerous cut marks, likely to facilitate binding to a projectile point. Several pieces of chokecherry wood and sagebrush cordage were also recovered in cultural layer 34, indicating that wooden implements and textiles were manufactured at the site.

Mummy Cave's Late Archaic occupations show remarkable consistency with the preceding Early and Middle Archaic periods. It is clear that while bison hunting emerged in the Great Plains, upland hunter-gatherers continued to exploit a wide variety of other game during the Late Archaic.

SPRING CREEK CAVE

Spring Creek Cave, located in the Bighorn Mountains in north-central Wyoming, yielded a remarkable array of perishable items radiocarbon dated to approximately 1,800 years ago, providing an enormous amount of information regarding nonstone tool industries of Late Archaic hunter-gatherers. Among the more important artifacts were wooden atlatl handles and foreshafts, a few with attached Pelican Lake projectile points. The dryness of the cave preserved a wide variety of other perishable items, including wooden digging sticks and projectiles, and textiles including travois and basketry fragments. The perishable artifacts from Spring Creek Cave show their makers' remarkable knowledge of the flora and fauna of northern Wyoming and indicate a way of life deeply embedded in mobile hunting and gathering. It is because of Spring Creek Cave that we infer that most Archaic notched projectile points were utilized as part of a multicomponent atlatl dart-hunting technology. This cave site, along with Mummy Cave on the Shoshone River and Wedding of the Waters Cave near Thermopolis, provides a rare glimpse into another part of the Great Plains hunter-gatherer world—a world that goes well beyond that of stone tools and bison bone.

OBSIDIAN CLIFF

In 1995, Leslie Davis of Montana State University and colleagues provided a chronology of use of Obsidian Cliff, an extremely important resource in Yellowstone National Park. One of the most intensive periods of Obsidian Cliff use was approximately 2,000 years ago, during the Late Archaic, when the cliff was used to supply eastern peoples. Early to Middle Woodland (Hopewell) Cultures of the Ohio River valley and into Wisconsin and the southern Great Plains engaged in trade and possibly

Obsidian at Obsidian Cliff, Wyoming

even long-distance travel to Obsidian Cliff to procure large quantities of obsidian. Evidence for this includes the presence of more than 660 pounds of obsidian at a single Hopewell site in Ohio, alongside the remains of bighorn sheep, which are native to the Rocky Mountains. Design motifs on Hopewell pottery indicate that individuals may have witnessed and hunted these animals themselves.

During the Late Archaic, large quarry pits were dug on the top of the cliff. There, miners hand excavated large, pristine cobbles of the rare natural glass. In a detailed analysis of obsidian distribution throughout the Great Plains, Leslie Davis found that Late Archaic Pelican Lake cultures account for 18.3 percent of the total procurement at Obsidian Cliff, second only to the Late Prehistoric Old Women's Culture (32.6 percent).

The Era of Buffalo Hunters and Villages

◄──────────────────────────────►
The Late Prehistoric Period
1,500 TO 300 YEARS AGO

While the Late Plains Archaic period marked the emergence of a bison-hunting culture in the Great Plains, the Late Prehistoric period—1,500 to 300 years ago—can be defined as a time in which bison hunting reigned supreme all over the northern Great Plains. Bison hunting escalated in intensity, with many more locations used for hunts, many more individuals participating in the complex organization of bison hunting, and many more bison being hunted in comparison to the Late Archaic. Instead of dozens of animals at a bison jump as during the Late Archaic, Late Prehistoric bison kills often have hundreds of animals. Archaeologists found the remains of as many as twenty thousand bison at the Vore Buffalo Jump in Wyoming. Hundreds of buffalo jumps in Montana date to the Late Prehistoric period.

John Fisher and Tom Roll of Montana State University compared Late Archaic bison hunting data to Late Prehistoric data for Montana archaeological sites. In addition to showing bigger sites with more bison killed in the Late Prehistoric, Fisher and Roll found that Late Prehistoric hunters were much more active during all seasons of the year. Several sites show use throughout the year. Fisher and Roll also note that Late Prehistoric hunters were more intensive in bison carcass processing compared to Late Archaic hunters.

Increased numbers of stone circles, buffalo kill sites, and Late Prehistoric arrow points suggest that the human population increased during the Late Prehistoric period in the Great Plains region. The population increase may have been due to the heightened intensity of hunting for bison and other animals, or it may be the reason for it. The population increase probably led to increased territoriality and heightened use of all varieties of animals and plants within each group's home territory. Certainly, the diverse suite of remains at the Vestal Site in Montana and Mummy Cave in Wyoming supports the conclusion that other plants and animals were exploited in addition to bison. In the Northwest and Great Plains, nomadic peoples began to settle down and live in permanent villages approximately 900 years ago. While such village sites are rare in

Montana, they are common to the Northwest in British Columbia and to the east along the Missouri River in North Dakota. In the Northwest, hunter-gatherers lived in villages during the fall and winter, while Missouri River villagers in the Dakotas were agriculturalists, harvesting corn, beans, and squash to trade with bison hunters in Montana and Wyoming. The emergence of permanent villages marks an important first for the Late Prehistoric period. Prior to this time, denizens of the Great Plains and Rocky Mountains were hunter-gatherers. While most people in Montana continued to hunt and gather for subsistence throughout the Late Prehistoric period, they certainly were influenced by villagers to the east and west who opted for a more settled lifestyle.

Pictograph Cave and Ghost Cave near Billings, excavated as part of the Works Progress Administration jobs program in the late 1930s, generated many remarkable finds dating to the Late Prehistoric period, including a human face effigy stone, a turtle pendant, a knife hafted to a handle, a bison scraper, and perishable items. Among the most noteworthy perishable items is basketry so tightly woven that it was likely used

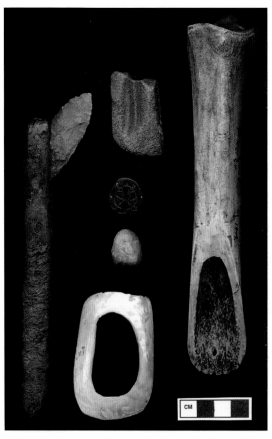

Pictograph Cave and Ghost Cave artifacts, clockwise from far left: hafted knife, sandstone abrader, bison bone scraper, shell pendant, face effigy, and turtle pendant
—Courtesy of Montana State Parks, a division of Montana Fish, Wildlife, and Parks

Pictograph Cave near Billings

to carry water approximately 900 years ago. Unfortunately, the lack of excavation details makes analysis of these sites difficult, so they are not included in my site descriptions.

The Bow and Arrow

The Late Prehistoric period witnessed a major first: the adoption of the bow and arrow in Montana approximately 1,500 years ago, facilitating the hunting of bison, deer, elk, and other game. This innovative technology allowed for the use of smaller projectile points that were more easily produced in bulk and did not necessarily require large pieces of high-quality stone. This was particularly useful for bison hunters, who frequently traveled away from sources of high-quality stone in pursuit of bison herds. Use of Knife River Flint decreased substantially between the Late Archaic and Late Prehistoric periods, while use of Obsidian Cliff obsidian increased slightly.

The bow and arrow also allowed for clandestine firing from behind protective cover, improving the odds when hunting. The atlatl of the Archaic period required firing from a standing position, effectively forcing the hunter to reveal himself during the attack.

Because of the widespread benefits of the bow and arrow, hunters from all over the Great Plains and Rocky Mountains quickly adopted it. While Besant atlatl points continued to be used in some areas until about 1,300 years ago, they completely disappear after that. The reason we know the date of this transition so well is that Late Prehistoric arrow points,

125

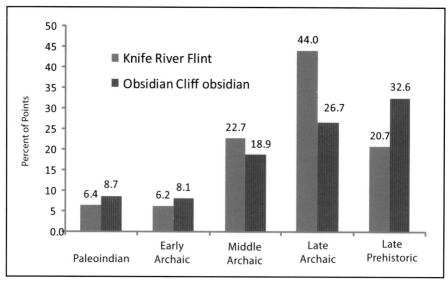

The percentage of points made from obsidian from Obsidian Cliff increased in the Late Prehistoric period compared to early periods, while the percentage of points made from Knife River Flint decreased compared to the Late Archaic.
—Data from Ahler, 1986, and Davis and others, 1995

Late Prehistoric obsidian points found near Yellowstone Lake in Wyoming

which are found in the hundreds and thousands at Late Prehistoric sites, are easy to identify because of their small size and are only found at sites younger than 1,500 years ago. Late Prehistoric arrow points are on average half the size, and sometimes a quarter of the size, of Archaic atlatl points. Some Late Prehistoric points are the size of a fingernail.

Approximately 1,500 years ago, hunter-gatherers began using the Avonlea arrow point in Montana and the surrounding region. This arrow point was finely manufactured, with very shallow side or corner notches, a convex to straight blade, and a slightly concave base. Avonlea points

Late Prehistoric arrow points from Ghost Cave near Billings —Courtesy of Montana State Parks, a division of Montana Fish, Wildlife, and Parks

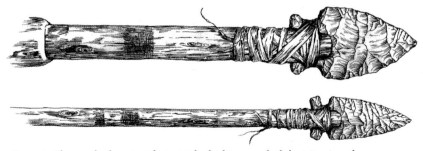

Besant side-notched projectile point hafted to an atlatl dart (top) and Avonlea point hafted to arrow (bottom). Note the difference in size.
—Courtesy of Nathan Goodale; Eric Carlson illustration

are a transitional point type between the larger Archaic atlatl point and the very small arrow point introduced approximately 1,300 years ago. With the exception of the Avonlea arrow point, Late Prehistoric arrow points generally are not as finely manufactured as their atlatl counterparts and were frequently produced using low- to medium-grade stone.

Between approximately 1,200 and 300 years ago, the predominant style of point is the Late Prehistoric side-notched point. While some regional archaeologists describe a large variety of these arrow points, the overall form is similar, with diversity seen in notching and the shape of the blade and base. The typical point has shallow side notches and a straight base. Arrow point blades are typically straight to slightly convex, with a triangular shape. Just before contact with European-Americans in the eighteenth century, some Late Prehistoric hunters added a third notch to the bases of their projectile points; these arrow points are sometimes referred to as Late Prehistoric tri-notch points.

Stone Circles

There are an estimated five to six million stone circles in the Great Plains, with several hundred thousand in Montana alone. The visibility of stone circles makes campsites easy to find. While there has been some debate as to the function of stone circles, the vast majority are the remains of house structures—today most commonly called tepees—used by mobile

*Stone circle and reconstructed tepee pole structure at
Lake Ilo National Wildlife Refuge in North Dakota*

hunter-gatherers of the Great Plains. The stones were used to weigh down the base of the hide coverings of the tepees when erected. When inhabitants prepared to leave a site, they pulled up the hides, leaving the stones behind. Stone circles may also mark the locations of other features, including medicine wheels or even sweat lodges, but the majority are house remains.

While they originated in the Middle Plains Archaic and experienced increased use in the Late Plains Archaic, tepees gained dominance during the Late Prehistoric period, the heyday of Great Plains bison hunting. These circular features measure approximately 10 to 20 feet in diameter. Stone circles are typically found near water and often are in protected settings with excellent views of the surrounding country. Stone circles found in fairly close proximity to bison kill sites mark the locations of base camps used during buffalo hunting.

Stone circles occasionally have central rock features, which most commonly are hearths. The presence of central hearths indicates possible use during cold weather, whereas hearths outside the structure indicate warm-weather use.

Pottery

The Late Prehistoric period witnessed a significant increase in the use of pottery, although it remains comparatively rare in Montana sites. Pottery was especially used by those living in or near permanent villages, and bison hunters in Montana were highly mobile people, preferring more portable basketry and leather for transporting goods. The Hagen Site, the only well-excavated Late Prehistoric permanent village site in Montana, yielded thousands of pottery sherds.

Many types of pottery were made by Late Prehistoric peoples, but three main styles are predominant in archaeological assemblages in Montana: Avonlea pottery, Intermountain (Shoshone) pottery, and Crow pottery. Avonlea pottery is among the earliest styles in Montana, preceded only by Besant pottery of the Late Archaic period. Dating to approximately 1,500 to 1,000 years ago, Avonlea pottery is globular in shape, tempered with grit and impressed with a net-type pattern and/or grooved exterior design. Avonlea pottery is most commonly found in the northern portion of Montana, particularly in the northeast, as well as in North Dakota and southern Alberta and Saskatchewan.

Intermountain, or Shoshone, pottery was made by Shoshone groups from Wyoming and Utah approximately 1,200 years ago. Primarily found at sites in northern Wyoming and, more rarely, southern Montana, it is also globular but features flanged bases and flat bottoms and lacks rim treatment. Exterior and interior surfaces of Intermountain pottery are smooth. It is often found in association with vessels carved from soapstone.

CEREMONIAL AND BIOGRAPHIC ROCK ART TRADITIONS

Two important rock art traditions—Ceremonial and Biographic—found expression in the Late Prehistoric period at sites all over the northern Great Plains, with some of the best examples in Montana. The Ceremonial Tradition was produced between 1,100 and 400 years ago, and the Biographic Tradition was produced between 400 and 200 years ago. The artists were people of a variety of tribal affiliations, including ancestral Blackfeet, Crow, and Northern Cheyenne.

The Ceremonial Tradition, painted or pecked on rock faces, depicts humans with and without shields. Less commonly, V-neck figurines without shields have rectangular bodies, round heads, and stick arms and legs. More common are shield-bearing warriors—V-neck figurines depicted with large, full-body shields. The shields carry colorful insignias important to the individuals, perhaps representing tribal, clan, band, or warrior-society affiliation. Bear Gulch in central Montana has more shield-bearing warriors—hundreds of them—than all of the other Ceremonial rock art sites in the northern Great Plains combined. Many of the shield-bearing warriors are shown with headdresses and ceremonial staffs with tassels, probably indicating dances and other festivities. We know that the shield-bearing warriors were produced before the introduction of the horse; shields during the horse era were much smaller than during the pre-horse era due to the difficulty of riding with a large shield. Important Ceremonial Tradition rock art sites include Bear Gulch and Pictograph Cave in Montana, Castle Gardens and Medicine Lodge Creek in Wyoming, and Writing-on-Stone in Alberta, Canada.

Beginning about 400 years ago, Native Americans stopped producing shield-bearing warriors and switched to producing rock art of the Biographic Tradition.

Shield-bearing warriors of the Ceremonial Tradition at Bear Gulch in Montana
—John Greer photo

This art was produced in many of the same locations as Ceremonial art and was likely produced by the same people. However, for some reason the emphasis of the art switched from shield-bearing warriors to realistic historical and biographic representations either painted or pecked into rock. Pictograph Cave in Billings is the most famous biographic rock art site in Montana. Writing-on-Stone in far southern Alberta has some of the tradition's best examples. Writing-on-Stone is located among dramatic hoodoo landforms along the Milk River. Biographic scenes typically depict acts of war or heroism. The art shows men in battle and riding horses, and objects such as tepees and wagons. Some biographic art panels depict entire battles.

Shield-bearing warrior of the Ceremonial Tradition at Medicine Lodge Creek in Wyoming

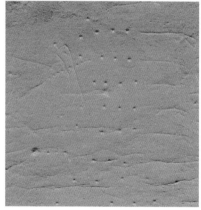

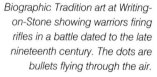

Biographic Tradition art at Writing-on-Stone showing warriors firing rifles in a battle dated to the late nineteenth century. The dots are bullets flying through the air.

The landscape at Writing-on-Stone in southern Alberta

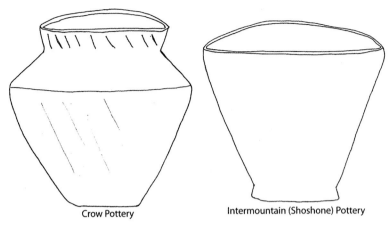

Crow Pottery   Intermountain (Shoshone) Pottery

Schematic illustrations of Crow pottery and Intermountain (Shoshone) pottery

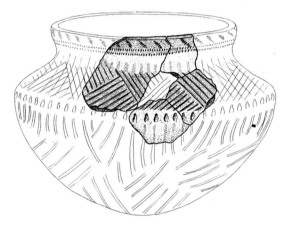

Illustrated reconstruction of a Crow pottery vessel from the Hagen Site in eastern Montana —University of Montana Anthropology Collections; William Mulloy illustration

Some sites in Yellowstone National Park and southwestern Montana have yielded Intermountain pottery, suggesting use of these landscapes by Shoshone peoples moving northward from the Great Basin and Wyoming in the last 1,000 years.

Crow pottery was introduced to Montana from the Dakotas approximately 500 years ago. About this time, the Crow split from the Hidatsa and left the Missouri River valley of North Dakota to become bison hunters in the open plains of Montana and northern Wyoming. Crow pottery has grit temper, a globular form with an S-shaped rim, and a smooth exterior and interior. Parallel incised lines and small dots formed by pointed depressions are common decorations, and incised lines are also common on rims. It resembles Hidatsa and Mandan pottery, further solidifying the ancestral roots of the Crow.

Crow pottery —University of Montana Anthropology Collections

Shoshone pottery sherds from Pictograph Cave near Billings —Courtesy of Montana State Parks, a division of Montana Fish, Wildlife, and Parks

The presence of pottery at Late Prehistoric sites allows archaeologists to more accurately link the sites to specific tribal groups. If pottery is recovered, it often can be attributed to the Shoshone or the Crow, effectively marking their presence at the site. Prior to the Late Prehistoric, there are few artifact types that allow archaeologists to infer the ethnicity of site occupants.

Late Prehistoric Villages

Montana is one of the few states that was largely devoid of agriculture and permanent villages during the Late Prehistoric period. Montana's cold temperatures, short growing season, and unpredictable precipitation discouraged agriculture. With reliable sources of wild plants and animals to eat, most inhabitants of Montana chose to hunt and gather.

Permanent villages did emerge in the Dakotas, all along the banks of the Missouri River. During the Late Prehistoric period, major tribes including the Mandan and Hidatsa in North Dakota and the Arikara in South Dakota possessed an economy based on corn agriculture. Villagers traded for meat, hides, and other goods with Montana bison hunters, though they also did their own hunting to supplement their crops. The earliest such villages sprouted along the Missouri River approximately 1,100 years ago and increased in number between 700 and 500 years ago. These villages were present at the time of European-American contact, as illustrated by artist George Catlin in the early nineteenth century. In 1994, Peter Winham and Edward Lueck reported the remains of nearly one hundred Missouri River villages in North and South Dakota. While these villages were certainly not all occupied at the same time, the large number suggests a fairly high population density, on the order of thousands of inhabitants at any given moment along the Missouri River in the Dakotas.

Villages such as Double Ditch north of Bismarck, North Dakota, were built on high terraces overlooking the Missouri River and its tributaries in the Dakotas. Over time, with increasing populations and corresponding territorial skirmishes, some villages were fortified with moats and walls. Tensions between tribes likely escalated because of competition over limited resources.

One of the most gruesome of all Late Prehistoric village sites is the Crow Creek Site in South Dakota. The site dates to approximately 700 years ago, thus preceding European-American contact in the area. At

A ditch, the remains of a security measure to protect the village from invaders, at the Double Ditch village site along the Missouri River in North Dakota

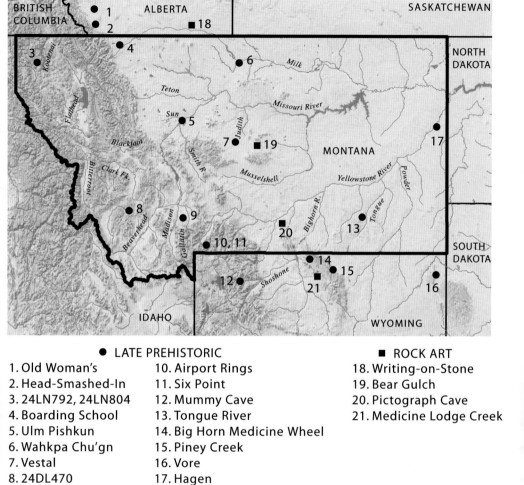

● LATE PREHISTORIC   ■ ROCK ART

1. Old Woman's
2. Head-Smashed-In
3. 24LN792, 24LN804
4. Boarding School
5. Ulm Pishkun
6. Wahkpa Chu'gn
7. Vestal
8. 24DL470
9. Madison

10. Airport Rings
11. Six Point
12. Mummy Cave
13. Tongue River
14. Big Horn Medicine Wheel
15. Piney Creek
16. Vore
17. Hagen

18. Writing-on-Stone
19. Bear Gulch
20. Pictograph Cave
21. Medicine Lodge Creek

Late Prehistoric sites in Montana and the surrounding region

Crow Creek, archaeologists uncovered the bodies of 486 individuals—mostly adult males—within a burial pit. All of the skeletons showed extensive trauma associated with a battle. The low numbers of women and children suggest that they were taken by the invaders. Although the bodies were found in a burial pit, they apparently had lain on the ground surface for an extended period; scavenger marks were found on many of the bodies. They may have been buried by another group who arrived at the site and decided to use it for their own village.

Hunter-gatherers also witnessed increased violence during the Late Prehistoric period. In 2006, Indiana University archaeologist Laura Scheiber reported that "projectile points are embedded in bone of 17 percent of individuals dating to the Late Prehistoric compared to no known incidences from previous periods."

The Columbia Plateau witnessed the emergence of permanent villages during the Late Prehistoric period, approximately 1,200 to 500 years ago. While no such villages have been identified in the archaeological record of western Montana, many were probably present along rivers in the Columbia River Basin, including the Clark Fork, Kootenai, and Flathead rivers. In British Columbia, at Bridge River and Keatley Creek villages, Anna Prentiss and her students from the University of Montana have identified salmon-fishing villages that were used by hundreds of individuals likely organized into complex chiefdoms with a high degree of social stratification. The sheer quantity of salmon in these areas allowed for resource ownership with differential access to fishing locations, thus increasing social stratification. Villagers lived in pit houses, and modern excavation of these provided an intimate window into the lives of Late Prehistoric salmon villagers not far from Montana.

HAGEN SITE

The Hagen Site, among the most important sites ever excavated in Montana, was a permanent village located north of Glendive in Dawson County on the Yellowstone River. The Nollmeyer Site, a short distance downstream, is the only other excavated permanent village site in Montana. Excavations at the Hagen Site were conducted in the late 1930s under the direction of William Mulloy and Oscar Lewis, the same pair that teamed up to complete excavations at Pictograph Cave near Billings. The Hagen Site is possibly linked to the Crow-Hidatsa schism, when the Crow departed western North Dakota approximately 800 to 500 years ago to become bison hunters in Montana and Wyoming. The Crow language is closely related to that of the Hidatsa, suggesting that the split occurred recently. Another possible interpretation is that the Hagen Site was a Hidatsa village used as a base camp for hunting bison, which they then transported back to their villages in the Dakotas. Unlike similar permanent villages in North Dakota, the Hagen Site yielded more than 340 bison, indicating that its occupants hunted and processed bison.

Dated to approximately 600 years ago, the site yielded nearly thirty thousand pottery sherds from the production of Crow vessels. Along with the Crow pottery, hundreds of Late Prehistoric side- and tri-notched arrow points were recovered at the site.

The site resembles a Hidatsa village, including a circular earth lodge, a mound, storage pits, and human burials. An earth lodge is a semisubterranean shelter that has a dome roof covered with earth. As described in Mulloy's 1942 site report, the earth lodge at the Hagen Site measured approximately 16 feet in diameter and had a shallow, 5-inch-deep excavated floor. The lodge was almost perfectly circular, with twelve interior post holes, averaging 4 to 5 inches in diameter, that held structural timbers. The interior floor of the lodge was hard packed by intensive use and an entrance to the house was attached to the east. The center of the lodge contained a fire pit and a pile of ash aligned next to two posts, probably evidence of a central fire and a central standing support system for the house. This earth lodge resembles those historically used by the Mandan and Hidatsa in North Dakota.

A few hundred feet north of the lodge was a 45-foot-wide, perfectly circular mound. The sides of the mound sloped up to a flat top that stood approximately 4 to 5 feet above the ground. Within the mound, Mulloy recovered an extensive bone midden, primarily composed of human bones, especially mandibles (jaws). Other artifacts in the mound included stone artifacts and pottery. Based on the human remains, Mulloy interpreted it to be a burial mound.

Another significant feature at the Hagen Site is the abundance of storage pits scattered across the site. One type of storage pit was bell shaped, while another form was basket shaped. The pits were excavated into the subsurface clay, and finger marks were discernible along the edges of the pits. Some of the pits were as large as 6 feet in diameter and completely filled with dense layers of artifacts and soil. During use of the village, these pits likely were utilized to store food, but upon abandonment of the site they were filled with refuse.

Reconstructed house structure at Knife River Indian Villages National Historic Site in North Dakota, similar to that used by residents of the Hagen Site in Montana

Late Prehistoric Sites in Western Montana

SITES 24LN792 AND 24LN804

In western Montana, the Kootenai, Flathead, Clark Fork, Blackfoot, and Bitterroot valleys were all extensively used during the Late Prehistoric period. These valleys provided outstanding water sources and also served as travel corridors to high-quality root-collecting and hunting grounds. Alston Thoms's 2006 archaeological surveys near Libby have identified several Late Prehistoric sites, likely indicating ancestral Kootenai and/or Salish occupations in the region. Two sites—24LN792 and 24LN804—are on high terraces overlooking the now-inundated Kootenai River at Lake Koocanusa. Radiocarbon dates on charcoal in hearths at both sites showed active use of the area by mobile hunter-gatherers between 900 and 500 years ago. Mammal remains—including deer, elk, and other medium and large mammals—were plentiful at the sites. Site 24LN804 yielded evidence of multiple cooking features. The sites indicate that deer hunting intensified during the Late Prehistoric period west of the Continental Divide, much as bison hunting increased east of the Divide. While northwest Montana deer hunting sites are common, they are sometimes difficult to find in this densely wooded portion of the state.

SITE 24DL470

Another important Late Prehistoric campsite is Site 24DL470 along the banks of the Big Hole River near the small town of Wise River. HRA of Missoula excavated the site in the early 2000s prior to construction on U.S. Highway 43. HRA excavated twenty-five test units across the site, yielding nearly two thousand stone artifacts. Late Prehistoric side-notched projectile points were recovered in association with radiocarbon-dated features, placing the occupation between 1,500 and 500 years ago. Much of the stone was obsidian from Bear Gulch, south of the site on the Idaho-Montana state line. Additional obsidian came from the Snake River Plain of Idaho, with sources including Timber Butte, Malad, and American Falls, as well as from Obsidian Cliff in Yellowstone National Park in Wyoming. These facts indicate strong connections between hunter-gatherers of southwestern Montana and people living in the northern Great Basin of southern Idaho.

Buffalo Hunting and Processing Sites

WAHKPA CHU'GN BUFFALO JUMP

In addition to its Late Archaic Besant occupation, the Wahkpa Chu'gn Buffalo Jump in Havre yielded the remains of several different Late Prehistoric visits to the site. The earliest was by hunters wielding Avonlea projectile points approximately 1,200 years ago. A few small fire hearths with fire-cracked rock and small bison-processing areas are the only evidence of this comparatively brief Avonlea occupation.

Following the Avonlea occupation, other groups wielding Late Prehistoric side-notched arrow points used the site intensively until about 600 years ago, according to John Brumley, the site excavator and museum curator. They drove bison down a steep slope along the Milk River and into a pound or corral. Brumley reported that the corral likely burned and was repaired at least twice. Hundreds of bison were dispatched in the corral on multiple occasions, primarily during the spring and fall.

Bison bone midden at Wahkpa Chu'gn Buffalo Jump in Havre

Roasting pits used in pemmican processing at Wahkpa Chu'gn Buffalo Jump in Havre

Secondary processing areas mark the locations where people prepared meat for transport. Burn features within the bison kill area, as well as intentional breakage of long bones to obtain bone marrow, indicate that pemmican was produced here.

FIRST PEOPLES BUFFALO JUMP

First Peoples Buffalo Jump, formerly called Ulm Pishkun, is a state park with a museum and hiking trails southwest of Great Falls. The site epitomizes the Great Plains buffalo jump, with a wide-open bison-gathering basin above the jump littered with rock cairns used in the bison drive. The jump stands about 20 feet tall and stone circles are scattered around its base. Unfortunately, in the early twentieth century Frost Fertilizer Company used heavy machinery to collect bones to be shipped to west coast cities for use in gardening. This practice was common at bison jump sites, resulting in the unfortunate disturbance of many important bison kill sites in Montana. Nevertheless, Ulm Pishkun has yielded significant and intact archaeological remains. In the mid-1990s, under the sponsorship of the Montana Department of Fish, Wildlife, and Parks, John Fisher, Tom Roll, and Steve Aaberg of Montana State University conducted excavations in three different locations along the cliff face at Ulm Pishkun. The archaeologists identified extensive bison bone beds, which indicate the running of hundreds of bison over the cliff.

First Peoples Buffalo Jump near Great Falls

Late Prehistoric arrow points, including Avonlea and Old Women's types, dominate the stone artifact assemblage, supporting the conclusion that the site primarily functioned as a kill location. Numerous projectile points were recovered in these bone beds, indicating that many bison likely survived the fall over the cliff and that hunters waited with arrows ready for the final kill shots. Although most of the projectiles were made from local stone, nearly a third were produced from obsidian, in all likelihood from Obsidian Cliff in Yellowstone National Park or Bear Gulch on the Montana-Idaho state line south of Dillon.

Radiocarbon dates from the site indicate that Native Americans used the excavated areas of the site between 1,000 and 500 years ago. By analyzing the stage of tooth eruption on juvenile bison, Fisher determined that the animals were killed in the fall, the most common time for bison hunts in Montana. This was the season for resource preparation prior to moving to winter camps. Hunts at Ulm Pishkun also occurred from late winter to early spring, as indicated by the recovery of unborn (fetal) bison bone in the archaeological excavations.

Primary processing of the animals took place at the base of the cliff where the animals were killed. Portions of the animals were then transported a short distance to secondary processing camps, where jerky and pemmican were made. These camps must have bustled with activity, and stone circles and other features mark the locations of tepees and activity areas.

Primary processing of bison occurred at the base of the Ulm Pishkun Buffalo Jump

*Tepee replicas at Ulm Pishkun, mimicking the camp
locations where people lived during their bison kills*

In addition to evidence of bison bone processing, the camps at Ulm Pishkun yielded a diverse suite of tools, including hide-processing tools and pottery, suggesting that whole families were present at the site for extended periods of time. They processed bison hides for use in a variety of important goods, including clothes and tepee covers. The presence of snake, bird, fox, coyote, rodent, rabbit, and pronghorn bones, as well as goosefoot (chenopodium) plant remains, also confirms that people were at the site for some time prior to and following the actual bison kill, perhaps preparing the bison drive lines and organizing people for their roles in the ensuing bison jump.

MADISON BUFFALO JUMP

Madison Buffalo Jump, a Montana state park south of Three Forks, has an excellent visitor center and trails extending up the face of the buffalo jump and out onto the top of the gathering basin. The site, located within a mile of the Madison River, was used during the Late Prehistoric period. Excavations were conducted by Carling Malouf and Dee Taylor of the University of Montana in the 1960s and 1970s. Unfortunately, results of these field operations are not widely available. In project notes at the University of Montana archives, Malouf describes disturbances at the site, likely due to mining of the main bison bone bed during the early twentieth century. As at Ulm Pishkun, several stone circles are present on the flat area below the main jump, probably indicating camp sites and secondary bison-processing areas.

A stone circle at the base of Madison Buffalo Jump south of Three Forks

Madison Buffalo Jump south of Three Forks

TONGUE RIVER BISON JUMP

A team from the University of Montana excavated the Tongue River Bison Jump in southeastern Montana in the late 1990s under the direction of Anna Prentiss and Tom Foor. The site is located near the town of Lame Deer on the Northern Cheyenne Indian Reservation, approximately 2 miles from the Tongue River on a small tributary stream. The jump was used approximately 1,100 years ago, based on radiocarbon dating of bison bone. Two areas of the site were identified: the bone bed and a

Tongue River Bison Jump near Lame Deer —Anna Prentiss photo

nearby stone tool workshop. The University of Montana and Northern Cheyenne excavation team unearthed more than twenty thousand bone fragments, representing approximately fifteen bison and a number of medium-sized mammals (deer, pronghorn) and small mammals (rabbit). Thus, while bison was the focus of subsistence, Late Prehistoric peoples here hunted diverse game. High-utility legs and ribs were removed from the site for processing at another location. In addition, a majority of the bison were four to five years old, suggesting that the hunters also were careful in their selection of animals to kill.

VESTAL SITE

The Vestal Site, located in Fergus County in the very center of Montana, was excavated by Ethnoscience of Billings as part of a pipeline project and reported by Jacqueline Payette and colleagues in 2006. The bison kill site is along Coyote Creek within the Judith Basin and measures some 86,000 square yards. The Ethnoscience team excavated 473 test units, yielding multiple features with dates ranging from 1,800 to 885 years ago. In association with these features, the site yielded seventy-three Avonlea projectile points, indicating a substantial Late Prehistoric site occupation.

The site was utilized on multiple occasions during the Late Prehistoric period, especially in the spring when bison herds were plentiful in the area. Bison was the main focus of subsistence; remains of at least fifty-eight bison were recovered at the site. Less than 1 percent of the site has been excavated, suggesting that as many as eight thousand animals may have been processed at the site during the Late Prehistoric period. Other food remains are present as well, including large canids (dogs/wolves), deer, and mussel shell. In each of the excavated bone beds, skulls, vertebrae, and ribs are underrepresented, suggesting that the site was an initial processing location from which these valuable pieces were transported elsewhere. The site yielded additional evidence of bison processing, including the stacking of bone elements, suggesting a well-organized team of workers. Finally, in one area of the site (north of Coyote Creek), archaeologists recovered the remains of several bone-boiling and grease-extraction features, likely associated with pemmican manufacture. The Vestal Site fits many of the common conceptions about the Late Prehistoric period, including intensive and well-organized bison procurement and processing and the incorporation of other game in the diet.

BOARDING SCHOOL BISON DRIVE

Another important Late Prehistoric bison kill site is the Boarding School Bison Drive in northwestern Montana, 5 miles north of Browning on the Blackfeet Indian Reservation. As reported by Thomas Kehoe in 1967, the site is a classic Great Plains bison kill site, with multiple drive lines on the upland flat above a steep terrace. Once driven over the abrupt drop, the animals were trapped within a corral. Kehoe's archaeological work identified the remnants of the corral, including thirty wooden poles, each measuring 3 to 4 inches in diameter and 5 to 6 feet long. Wood used to build the structure included cherry, willow, eastern cottonwood, and aspen. The corral posts were supported by vertically placed bones.

Kehoe estimates a minimum of 250 bison were killed and processed at Boarding School Bison Drive in approximately the year 1590. Dozens of Late Prehistoric side-notched arrow points were found at the site, along with many scraping and cutting tools used during the processing of bison. Probably utilized from late summer to fall, the site is one of many bison jumps in this region used by the ancestral Blackfeet during the Late Prehistoric period.

AIRPORT RINGS SITE

The Airport Rings Site, on an upland terrace within 300 feet of the Yellowstone River, is north of Gardiner in a portion of Yellowstone National Park called the Boundary Lands. A team from the University of Montana excavated three stone circles at the site, each of which contained Late Prehistoric occupations. Central hearths were identified in two of the stone circles and had charcoal that was radiocarbon dated to approximately 350 years ago.

Stone circle feature showing a central hearth with ash at the Airport Rings Site near Gardiner

Late Prehistoric projectile point, measuring 2.5 centimeters long, from the Airport Rings Site near Gardiner

One of the stone circles yielded an intensively used central fire hearth with ash distributed toward the northeast in the interior of the stone circle. The ash deposit indicates that a southwesterly wind blew through the tepee, pushing ash against its northeastern wall. Given that the hearth is interior to the circle, a family probably was caught in a cold-weather storm and had to burn a very hot fire inside the tepee, creating the deep layer of ash. A bison tooth found inside the central hearth indicates they ate bison. Stone used at the site includes obsidian from Obsidian Cliff in Yellowstone National Park in Wyoming and dacite from Grasshopper Knob in southwestern Montana. As reported by Michael Livers and myself in 2009, Airport Rings is likely a camp used by a small family returning from a hunting and gathering expedition to the Yellowstone Plateau, perhaps in late fall.

146

HEAD-SMASHED-IN BUFFALO JUMP

Head-Smashed-In Buffalo Jump in south-central Alberta yielded substantial Late Prehistoric occupations to go along with its Late Archaic Besant occupations discussed earlier. The Avonlea occupation shows the complex organizational skills used by that culture between approximately 1,800 and 1,150 years ago. The bone midden in the Avonlea occupation is 9 to 12 feet thick and had numerous Avonlea projectiles intermixed with the remains of approximately forty-one bison. The bison herd was composed of cows and young, which were killed by the Avonlea people during the fall.

In contrast to earlier occupations during the Late Archaic period, the Avonlea people did not import any stone from exotic locations to the south, instead obtaining stone from the west at sources in British Columbia. An overall increase in the use of local chert and quartzite in arrow point manufacture indicates that Late Prehistoric flintknappers understood that there was little need to get high-quality stone for the manufacture of small arrow points. Still, the Avonlea projectile points were finely manufactured, maintaining the Archaic quality that was lost in many of the later Late Prehistoric side-notched points.

Above the Avonlea occupation is a significant occupation of the Old Women's cultural complex, so named after the Late Prehistoric components at a nearby site. Use of the site by the Late Prehistoric Old Women's Culture persisted from 1,100 years ago to historic times. Two radiocarbon dates mark at least two major occupations at approximately 1,100 and 750 years ago. In all likelihood the site was used repeatedly during the entire Late Prehistoric period. The total number of bison taken during the Old Women's occupations is not established, but it was probably in the hundreds, if not thousands. Evidence of multiple burn episodes at the kill site suggests that carcasses were burned after processing so they wouldn't rot at the site and prevent future use.

Old Women's arrow points were not as finely manufactured as Avonlea points and are a variant of the Late Prehistoric side-notched variety. While most arrow points were produced from local stone, some smaller points were produced from exotic materials, including Obsidian Cliff obsidian, Knife River Flint, and Montana cherts and porcellanite. This suite of stone sources indicates trade ties to populations to the south.

OLD WOMAN'S BUFFALO JUMP

The Old Woman's Buffalo Jump, some 50 miles north of Head-Smashed-In Buffalo Jump in Alberta, contained one of the most substantial Late Prehistoric occupations recorded at any buffalo jump in the northern Great Plains. Hundreds of Late Prehistoric side-notched arrow points were recovered here in association with the remains of hundreds of bison. Richard Forbis's 1960 description of the Old Women's cultural complex is based on this site.

147

VORE BUFFALO JUMP

The Vore Buffalo Jump is one of the most substantial and interesting bison kill sites anywhere in the Great Plains. Investigated by Charles Reher and George Frison of the University of Wyoming, the site is located along a small tributary of Spearfish Creek in the Bear Lodge Mountains of northwestern Wyoming, some 33 miles south of the Montana state line and 5 miles west of the South Dakota state line. The jump is unique in its structure: it does not entail driving bison over a cliff per se but instead utilizes a natural sinkhole within an otherwise vast, wide-open prairie. Imagine a charging herd of bison suddenly disappearing into a huge hole in the earth, with hunters waiting to ambush them from a safe hiding spot.

The sinkhole measures 125 feet across and 50 feet deep, and the bottom is layered approximately 15 to 20 feet deep with bison bones. Radiocarbon dates place use of the Vore Buffalo Jump between 320 and 250 years ago. Based on the size of the sinkhole and the depth of the bones, Reher and Frison estimate a minimum of ten thousand bison—and possibly as many as twenty thousand—were killed at the this site. Studies of the bison bone indicate use of the site throughout the year, further confirmation that Late Prehistoric bison hunting was a full-time endeavor.

Stone tools used at Vore were largely made from local sources in the Black Hills but also include porcellanite from southeastern Montana, Knife River Flint from western North Dakota, and Spanish Diggings quartzite from sources 150 miles south of the site. Reher and Frison infer that the predominance of these materials reflects influxes of Native Americans of differing ethnicities using the site as they moved through the region.

GLENROCK BUFFALO JUMP

The Glenrock Buffalo Jump, located in central Wyoming along the North Platte River, is a 6-mile-long and 30- to 50-foot-tall escarpment. Bison were pushed for between 1 and 3 miles to the edge of the escarpment, where they were run off the cliff using drive lines. Only a small number of projectiles were recovered here, likely because the long fall killed animals on impact. At least fifteen stone circles are present along the base of the cliff near the kill site and mark the locations of camps used by Native Americans during the hunts.

Radiocarbon dating of the bison bone bed indicates its use at the end of the Late Prehistoric period, approximately 300 years ago. As with most bison kill sites, initial processing of prime pieces—leg bones, ribs, and skulls—occurred on-site, and then these key portions were transported to secondary locations for further preparation. Glenrock Buffalo Jump's main season of use was fall.

PINEY CREEK BUFFALO JUMP

The Piney Creek Buffalo Jump in north-central Wyoming is located on the floodplain of Piney Creek on the eastern flank of the Bighorn Mountains. Similar to the Boarding School Bison Drive in Montana and the Vore Buffalo Jump in Wyoming, Piney Creek is not a cliff jump but is instead a drive over an abrupt drop, here from a high terrace onto a lower creek floodplain. A large number of projectile points at the Piney Creek site likely indicates that the escarpment was not steep enough to kill the animals. In all likelihood, a corral was used to capture the bison, although no structural remains were recovered during excavations. George Frison, who excavated the site, estimates that as many as 120 people occupied the site at any given time during the Late Prehistoric period, resulting in the accumulation of approximately two hundred bison. A single radiocarbon date places one occupation at 370 years ago.

Frison's team identified a large bison-processing area approximately 150 feet downstream from the kill site, with a campsite and several stone circles located approximately a quarter mile farther downstream. Pottery of the Crow style was recovered at Piney Creek, linking it to the Crow Tribe.

Pronghorn Hunting Sites

BRIDGER ANTELOPE TRAP

The Bridger Antelope Trap confirms that complex organizational skills during the Late Prehistoric period were not restricted to bison hunts. The Bridger Antelope Trap is located near the small town of Fort Bridger in Uinta County in southwestern Wyoming. Here, pronghorn were driven to the top of a small mesa, where the animals were trapped in a wooden post structure measuring approximately 1,500 by 600 feet. An 1,800-foot-long drive line was used to push the pronghorn onto the hilltop and into the trap. Juniper timbers are still extant on the hilltop, suggesting that the site was likely used as recently as the last 300 to 200 years, with earlier periods of use as well.

EDEN FARSON

Another pronghorn processing site, Eden Farson, located near the Green River valley of southwest Wyoming, is probably affiliated with the Shoshone because flat-bottomed Intermountain pottery was found there. Approximately 230 years ago, more than two hundred pronghorn were killed and processed at Eden Farson, probably representing an entire herd of animals of all ages. The age distribution of the animals at the site resembles that found in a living herd.

University of Montana students excavating shovel test pits in glacial outwash channels that served as natural drive lines at the Six Point Site

SIX POINT SITE

At the Six Point Site in the Montana portion of Yellowstone National Park, hunters drove pronghorn upslope onto the top of a glacial moraine. Instead of building drive lines, they used natural channels in the glacial outwash to drive the game up to the top, where they were killed. More than fifteen Late Prehistoric arrow points were recovered atop the Six Point Site, suggesting active use of the landform as a hunting ground.

Bighorn Sheep Hunting Camps

Bighorn sheep were a major focus of Late Prehistoric hunter-gatherers living in the Yellowstone area and the Rocky Mountains. Wickiups, shelters resembling lean-tos or timber A-frame structures, were present all over this region and were likely used by Shoshone people, many of whom hunted bighorn sheep and other animals in high-elevation settings.

A wickiup. The photographer and individual are unknown, but the location is thought to be the Pryor Mountains of south-central Montana.
—University of Montana Anthropology Collections

150

On the eastern edge of the Yellowstone ecosystem near Cody, Wyoming, Mummy Cave has yielded extensive evidence of bighorn sheep procurement by all of its occupants from Late Paleoindians to the hunter-gatherers of the Late Prehistoric. In Mummy Cave's Late Prehistoric site levels—cultural layers 36, 37, and 38—a wide range of unique perishable items were recovered. Cultural layer 36 yielded thirty hearths and a wide variety of corner-notched arrow points and basket fragments.

In cultural layer 36, a male skeleton probably of Shoshone tribal affiliation was recovered and dated to approximately 1,300 years ago. The man was wrapped in a bighorn sheep robe and his hair was tied at the back with a feather and fur ornament. The site is called Mummy Cave because of this body. The skeleton was removed during excavations and

MEDICINE WHEELS

Medicine wheels are composed of a central rock cairn surrounded by lines of rocks arranged in the shape of the spokes and rim of a wheel. More than 135 of these structures have been recorded in the Great Plains. The features probably played important roles in ceremonies, dances, and prayers and may be associated with the summer solstice. The most famous of these medicine wheel features is the Big Horn Medicine Wheel in the Bighorn National Forest of north-central Wyoming. The location has been used at least since the Late Prehistoric period as a prayer site by numerous northern Great Plains tribes, including Crow, Sioux, Arapaho, Blackfeet, Cheyenne, Shoshone, and Cree.

Big Horn Medicine Wheel in Wyoming —Gregory R. Campbell photo

put on display for years at the Buffalo Bill Historical Center in Cody, Wyoming. The center later agreed to remove the remains from display out of sensitivity to the individual's Native American descendants.

Above layer 36, cultural layer 37 dated to 1,000 to 700 years ago and contained Avonlea-like points. Shoshone-style pottery was recovered from this level, along with coiled basketry that is similar to Shoshone styles from the Great Basin. Finally, cultural layer 38 yielded Late Prehistoric side-notched and tri-notched arrow points alongside Shoshone pottery. All three of the Late Prehistoric occupations at Mummy Cave contained bighorn sheep remains.

Late Prehistoric basket fragments from Mummy Cave in Wyoming — Courtesy of Buffalo Bill Historical Center, Cody, Wyoming; gift of Harold McCracken, Mummy Cave Collection; Jack Richard photo; PN.29.48.PA201-L7.

Late Prehistoric human remains (likely Shoshone) with bighorn sheep robe found in Mummy Cave, Wyoming —Courtesy of Buffalo Bill Historical Center, Cody, Wyoming; gift of Harold McCracken, Mummy Cave Collection; Jack Richard photo; PN.29.017.

Contemporary Tribes and Future Work

Ancestors of many contemporary Native American tribes, including the Salish, Kootenai, Blackfeet, Crow, and Shoshone, utilized Montana between 1,500 and 300 years ago. We can approximate Montana's tribal territories of about 500 years ago (just prior to European-American contact), but the ethnicity of the people who used archaeological sites in Montana is a large and controversial research topic that will keep archaeologists busy for generations to come.

Archaeological data from Old Woman's Buffalo Jump, Head-Smashed-In Buffalo Jump, and Boarding School Bison Drive show the Blackfeet were present in and around Montana as far back as the latter portion of the Archaic and into the Late Prehistoric period. The presence of Intermountain pottery at sites in southern Montana and northern Wyoming indicates that the Shoshone had reached Montana by the Late Prehistoric period. In their 2002 report on Mummy Cave, Wilfred Husted and Robert Edgar effectively argue that the Shoshone may have been in Montana much longer, based on consistent use of the site dating to before the Middle Archaic period. Crow peoples are also noted in Montana and Wyoming during the Late Prehistoric period at the Hagen Site in Montana and Piney Creek Buffalo Jump in northern Wyoming.

Many of the tribes in Montana used similar technologies to hunt and gather, so it is often difficult to associate stone artifacts with specific tribes. For example, a Late Prehistoric arrow point from the Kootenai River valley may be virtually identical to one found in the Yellowstone River valley, though the two sites were probably used by people of different tribal origins. As Sally Greiser wrote in 1994, "We don't understand how projectile points, as we categorize them, relate to human groups. . . . To address ethnicity with this partial deck is a nearly overwhelming challenge." As such, the following overviews of tribal origins are approximate and, in many cases, best-guess scenarios based on the archaeological, linguistic, and Native American studies completed to date. For more detail and ethnographic information, I recommend the Smithsonian Institution's *Handbook of North American Indians* Volume 13 (for habitants of the Great Plains), Volume 12 (Columbia Plateau), and Volume 11 (Great Basin). Another excellent source of information

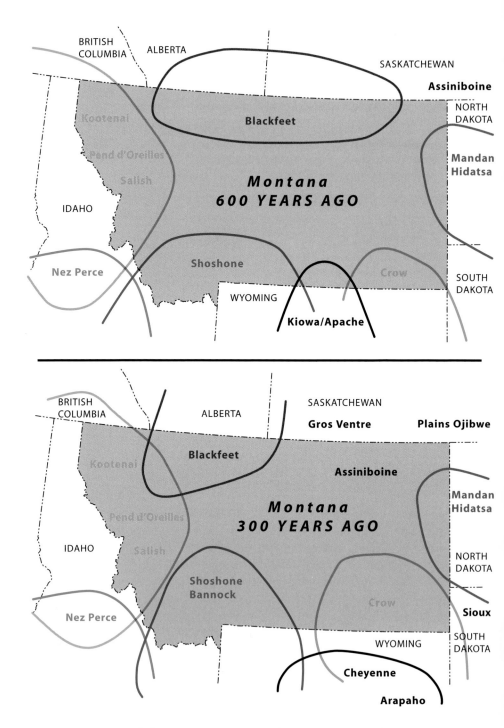

Approximate tribal territories in Montana about 600 years ago, before the intro-
duction of the horse, and about 300 years ago, after the introduction of the horse

on prehistoric evidence of tribal origins is Alan McMillan and Eldon Yellowhorn's *First Peoples in Canada*, as well as *Plains Indians, AD 500–1500: The Archaeological Past of Historic Groups*, edited by Karl Schlesier.

Tribal boundaries were greatly affected by the introduction of the horse to Montana in the early 1700s. The horse enabled many more tribes to travel to the state to participate in bison hunts. The horse also made Montana tribes more mobile, so their territories expanded. All of the Montana tribes obtained and used horses to facilitate mobility across the wide-open spaces of the Great Plains and Columbia Plateau. Tribal territories encountered by Lewis and Clark, for example, were probably somewhat different than during the prehorse Late Prehistoric period.

BLACKFEET ORIGINS

Ethnographic, linguistic, and archaeological data support Blackfeet presence in northwestern Montana for at least 2,000 years. Blackfeet origin stories point to an eastern origin within the last 2,000 years, and the Blackfeet language is similar to Algonquian dialects found in the northern Midwest. Archaeological sites may indicate even longer-term residence in northwest Montana and nearby areas, possibly extending back 3,000 years or more. For example, Head-Smashed-In Buffalo Jump in southern Alberta shows a sequence of occupations beginning in the Archaic period and continuing well into the Late Prehistoric period. Nevertheless, it is conceivable that the earliest Archaic occupations are associated with some other tribe, such as the ancestral Salish or Kootenai, and that the Blackfeet arrived during the Late Prehistoric period.

SALISH AND PEND D'OREILLES ORIGINS

The Salish and Pend d'Oreilles of western Montana have their roots to the west in the heart of the Columbia Plateau. They share an enormous amount of their culture, including similar languages, with other Salishan-speaking tribes in Idaho, Washington, British Columbia, and Oregon. Based on origin stories and archaeological information, it seems likely that the Salish in Montana have long held the region as the eastern edge of Salishan-speaking territories. There is no reason to believe that the Salish haven't been in western Montana since at least the early portion of the Archaic period. I don't think anyone would dispute the suggestion that the Salish are among the longest-tenured tribes in the northwestern Rocky Mountains. There is nothing in the archaeological record that points solidly to a specific time of origin for the Salish in Montana; nevertheless, based on continuity of use, the Salish likely have been in the region since the earliest peopling of the Americas.

KOOTENAI ORIGINS

While they now share a reservation—the Flathead—with the Salish and Pend d'Oreilles, and share numerous cultural traits with those tribes as well, the Kootenai of northwestern Montana and southern British Columbia and Alberta speak a language with no known similarities to those of other regional tribes. This indicates an ancient origin for the Kootenai, as does the consistent record of archaeological sites in northwest Montana from the Archaic period onward. Some archaeologists and anthropologists suggest that the Kootenai originated in the Montana Great Plains during the Archaic and eventually pushed west of the Continental Divide along with the Blackfeet and other tribes as they moved into central and northwestern Montana.

CREE-OJIBWE-ASSINIBOINE-GROS VENTRE ORIGINS

Today, the Cree, Ojibwe (Chippewa), Assiniboine, and Gros Ventre share reservations in far northeastern Montana as their tribal territory in Montana. These tribes also share a fairly recent arrival to the state, having come from the north and east within the last few hundred years. Linguistic and cultural similarities to tribes in Canada and the northern Midwest, as well as origin stories, support their use of the northern Montana Great Plains only within the last 500 years or so.

SHOSHONE ORIGINS

Among the most controversial origins of any Montana tribe is that of the Shoshone of southwestern Montana and northwestern Wyoming. While most archaeologists point to a fairly recent migration of the Shoshone out of the Great Basin within the last 1,000 years, some archaeological evidence points to a much longer period of occupation in the region. Certainly there was a push of Numic speakers out of the Great Basin within the last 1,500 to 1,000 years (Shoshone is a Numic language). The Shoshone could have been a part of that Numic spread, as suggested by many archaeologists. However, archaeological sites in the region—best exemplified by Mummy Cave in Wyoming—suggest that "sheep eaters," as the Shoshone are often called, have used the Shoshone River valley for the last 9,000 years. Mummy Cave has more than thirty cultural occupations starting at 9,000 years ago, with continuity of use into the current era. There is little doubt that the occupants of Mummy Cave for those nine millennia shared a similar subsistence and culture with each other.

It may be that the Shoshone traveled to the Yellowstone area during warm weather for hunting and gathering, returning to their Great Basin homeland during the cooler months. It seems likely that Numic speakers conducted northward pushes quite regularly during the last 9,000 years, with the classic Numic spread of 1,500 to 1,000 years ago being only the most recent and thus most visible in the archaeological record.

CROW ORIGINS

Compared to the Shoshone, Salish, Kootenai, and Blackfeet, the Crow are fairly recent migrants to Montana. Origin stories, linguistic similarities, and archaeological data all support a migration of the Crow out of a Hidatsa parent group within the last 800 to 500 years. The Crow and Hidatsa languages are very similar. Crow origin stories point to a split from the Hidatsa within fairly recent cultural memory. Archaeological sites, including the Hagen Site near Glendive, suggest movement out of the Hidatsa villages along the Missouri River in North Dakota and migration through eastern Montana to what is now their home territory in south-central Montana and northwestern Wyoming.

KIOWA-APACHE ORIGINS

Today, the Kiowa and Plains Apache live in the southern High Plains and Texas; however, Kiowa tradition indicates that their homeland is south-central Montana along the Yellowstone River. Their migration out of Montana probably was due to the introduction of the horse and the influx of other tribes, including the Shoshone and Crow, into the Montana Great Plains. The Kiowa and Plains Apache pushed southward and are reported to have been in the Black Hills in the early nineteenth century and in western Kansas, Oklahoma, and Texas by later in the nineteenth century.

Linguistically, the Kiowa are related to other groups in the American Southwest, including the Pueblo, while the Apache are linguistically affiliated with groups such as the Navajo. For the Kiowa, it is likely that their origins prior to 600 years ago were in the southwestern United States. For the Apache, their Athapaskan language ultimately suggests a northern origin in prehistory, but affiliation with other tribes in the American Southwest suggests long-term occupation there as well. Ultimately, the chronology of these movements for both the Kiowa and Apache is uncertain and difficult to infer from the archaeological record.

NORTHERN CHEYENNE ORIGINS

Like the Blackfeet of northwestern Montana, the Northern Cheyenne of southeastern Montana speak an Algonquian language. In *Plains Indians, AD 500–1500*, Karl Schlesier points to a common ancestral population of proto-Algonquian language speakers within the Great Lakes as the homeland of the Blackfeet and Cheyenne. He suggests that the Cheyenne pushed southwesterly into the Dakotas within the last 3,000 to 2,000 years, while the Blackfeet pushed westward into their current territories. It was only within the last few hundred years, with the advent of the horse, that the Northern Cheyenne came to be residents of Montana and the northwestern Great Plains.

OTHER TRIBES

Numerous other tribes have lived in Montana for a very long time as well, including the Nez Perce, Lakota Sioux, Mandan, Arapaho, Hidatsa, and Arikara. Most of these tribes hunted and gathered in Montana but spent most of their lives in surrounding areas. For example, the Nez Perce homeland is mostly to the west in Idaho and Oregon, but they are well known to have traveled to Montana to hunt bison in summer and fall.

Questions for Future Archaeologists

The study of the early human history of Montana covers a huge range of important archaeological research issues and key sites. The prehistory of Montana is unique among states in that it deals almost exclusively with hunter-gatherer populations. From the beginning of their time in Montana to the time of European-American contact, Montana's occupants were hunter-gatherers, unaffected by the emergence of agriculture and the social complexity that permanent villages bring. Montana is therefore an ideal place to study hunter-gatherer populations and their adaptations to their environment. Based on this overview of Montana's earliest occupants, various research questions arise relating to key discoveries at these sites:

Were the Clovis the first people in Montana? From where did they come?

What caused the megafaunal extinctions in Montana and the rest of the Americas?

Why did Folsom people flute their projectile points?

Why did later Paleoindians abandon the fluting technique used by the Folsom?

Did Folsom people gather in large groups on a seasonal basis?

Are Foothill/Mountain Paleoindian sites the product of the same people as lowland sites, or were the sites left by people of different cultures?

Why did people begin to use side-notched projectile points during the Early Archaic period?

How substantial was the population decline that occurred during the Altithermal, in the Early Archaic period?

Did Early Archaic people flee the open plains for the uplands during the Altithermal?

Did human populations increase after the Altithermal in the Early Archaic, along with bison populations?

Why do some sites show no evidence of bison hunting (for example, Mummy Cave), while others show it to be supremely important (for example, Wahkpa Chu'gn)?

How does rock art relate to hunting and gathering? For example, why do so few rock art sites show evidence of bison hunting?

Was access to stone quarries regulated by certain tribes, or was open access available to all peoples?

Do northwestern Montana archaeological sites contain evidence of fishing villages, as would be expected based on the archaeology of Washington, Idaho, and British Columbia?

Why did violence increase during the Late Prehistoric period in the Rockies and Great Plains?

How important was fishing to Montana hunter-gatherers?

How common were boats in Montana prehistory?

What inspired the change in Late Prehistoric rock art from the Ceremonial to Biographic styles?

Why did Montana populations increase during the Late Archaic period?

Appendix: Sites, Site Numbers, and Periods of Occupation

Site Name	Number	Period of Occupation*

UNITED STATES

COLORADO

Barger Gulch		Folsom
Jones-Miller		Hell Gap
Lindenmeier	5LR13	Folsom
Mahaffy		Clovis
Olsen-Chubbuck		Cody
Upper Twin Mountain		Goshen

IDAHO

Bear Gulch		obsidian
Simon	10CM7	Clovis

MONTANA

Airport Rings	24YE357	MPA, LPH
Antonsen	24GA660	LPA
Anzick Site	24PA506	Clovis
Avon Quarry	24PW263	chert
Barton Gulch	24MA171	Late Paleoindian
Bear Gulch	24FR2	LA, LP
Black Bear Coulee	24PW308	Agate Basin, EPA
Boarding School Bison Drive	24GL302	LPH
Buckeye	24CB1266	EPA, MPA
Carter Ferry Buffalo Jump	24CH1003	LPA
Cashman Quarry	24MA1618	dacite
Dodge	24RB1225	MPA
Eyebrow Quarry	24GN501	chert
Grady Ranch	24LC2013	dacite
Hagen	24DW1	LPH
Indian Creek	24BW626	Folsom, EPA
Keaster	24PH401	LPA
Keough Buffalo Jump	24ST401	LPA, LPH
King	24PH2886	Folsom
Kobold	24BH406	MPA, LPA
KXGN-TV	24DW79	Agate Basin/Hell Gap
Lime Creek Quarry	24GA1547	chert
Lindsay Mammoth	24DW501	Clovis
Logan Quarry	24GA400	chert
MacHaffie	24FJ0004	Folsom, Cody
Madison Buffalo Jump	24GA314	LPH
Mammoth Meadow	24BE559	Cody
Mill Iron	24CT30	Goshen
Mini-Moon	24DW85	LPA
Myers-Hindman	24PA504	EPA, MPA

Nollmeyer	24RL1225	LPH
Pictograph Cave	24YL0001	MPA, LPH
Powers-Yonkee	24PR5	MPA
Pretty Creek	24CB4	EPA
Rigler Bluffs	24PA401	MPA
RJP-1	24YE190	LPA
Schmitt Quarry	24BW559	LPA
Six Point	24YE170	LPH
Smith River Quarry	24ME69, 24ME232, 24ME467	chert
South Everson Creek Quarry	24BE559	chert
Spiro	24CB1332	MPA
Sun River	24CA74	MPA
Tongue River Bison Jump	24RB2135	LPH
Ulm Pishkun	24CA1012	LPH
Vestal	24FR760	LPH
Wahkpa Chu'gn Buffalo Jump	24HL101	LPA, LPH
Yellowstone Bank Cache	24YE357	LPA
No Name	24LN1054	EPA
No Name	24LN2210	MPA
No Name	24LN691	LPA
No Name	24LN792	LPH
No Name	24LN804	LPH
No Name	24DL470	LPH
No Name (Bear Paw Mtns.)	24HL1215	MPA

NEBRASKA

Hudson-Meng	25SX115	Cody

NORTH DAKOTA

Benz	32DU508	Cody
Big Black	32DU955	Folsom
Bobtail Wolf	32DU955	Folsom
Double Ditch	32BL8	LPH
Knife River Flint Quarries	32DU526	chert

OREGON

Paisley Caves		pre-Clovis

SOUTH DAKOTA

Beaver Creek Shelter	39CU779	EPA, MPA
Crow Creek	39BF11	LPH
Jim Pitts	39CU1142	Goshen
Lange-Ferguson	39SH33	Clovis
Licking Bison	39HN570	EPA
Lightning Spring	39HN204	MPA

WASHINGTON

Richey-Roberts (East Wenatchee)	45DO482	Clovis

WYOMING

Agate Basin	48NA201	Folsom
Bridger Antelope Trap	48UT1	LPH
Carter/Kerr-McGee	48CA12	Goshen, Folsom
Casper	48NA304	Hell Gap
Colby	48WA322	Clovis
Dead Indian Creek	48PA551	MPA
Fenn		Clovis
Fishing Bridge Point	48YE381	EPA, MPA
Glenrock Buffalo Jump	48CO304	LPH
Hawken	48CK303	EPA
Helen Lookingbill	48FR308	EPA
Hell Gap	48GO305	Goshen, Folsom, Hell Gap
Horner	48PA29	Cody
Lake Lodge Meadow	48YE1558	Cody
Leigh Cave	48WA304	MPA
McKean	48CK7	MPA
Medicine Lodge Creek	48BH499	Cody, EPA, MPA
Muddy Creek	48CR324	LPA
Mummy Cave	48PA201	Late Paleoindian, EPA, MPA, LPA, LPH
Obsidian Cliff	48YE433	LPA
Osprey Beach	48YE409	Cody
Piney Creek Buffalo Jump	48LO311	LPH
Ruby Bison Pound	48CA302	LPA
Sheaman	48NA211	Clovis
Spring Creek Cave	48WA1	LPA
Union Pacific		Clovis
Vore Buffalo Jump	48CK302	LPH

CANADA

ALBERTA

Cactus Flower	MPA
Head-Smashed-In Buffalo Jump	EPA, LPA, LPH
Kenney	LPA
Old Woman's Buffalo Jump	LPA, LPH
Wally's Beach	Clovis

BRITISH COLUMBIA

Bridge River	LPH
Keatley Creek	LPH

SASKATCHEWAN

Bracken Cairn	LPA
Long Creek Site	MPA, LPA
Mortlach	LPA
Sjovold	LPA

*EPA=Early Plains Archaic, MPA=Middle Plains Archaic, LPA=Late Plains Archaic, LPH=Late Prehistoric

Glossary

Altithermal. A hot, dry climatic period from about 8,000 to 5,000 years ago. It may have caused the extinction of *Bison antiquus* and led humans to diversify their subsistence.

andesite. A volcanic rock similar to basalt. Coarser than obsidian but still useful in stone tool manufacture.

antler rods. Tools made of bone and used by Clovis people in Montana 11,000 years ago. These rods may have been the foreshafts of atlatls.

arroyo. A dry creek bed with steep walls commonly used by hunter-gatherers to trap bison.

atlatl. A multicomponent spear-throwing device used by hunter-gatherers in Montana prior to 1,500 years ago. It is composed of a throwing board, or handle, with a long dart. A projectile point was hafted to a foreshaft, which then fit into the main shaft of the dart. Pronounced ät-lät-l.

awl. A pointed tool used for making holes in fabric and other materials.

basalt. A dark, iron- and magnesium-rich volcanic rock composed of lava cooled on the surface.

biface (bifacial). A stone tool produced by removing flakes from two sides of a stone, the goal being creation of a projectile point or knife.

bifurcate. A projectile point or knife with an indented (concave) base.

buffalo jump. A cliff face or other steep landform used by hunters to dispatch large numbers of bison by running them over the edge.

cache. A location where a large group of tools was left with the expectation of future use. Common to many time periods.

cairn. A pile of stones or rocks placed on the landscape for various reasons, such as to mark a trail or a burial location.

chalcedony. A translucent variety of chert used for stone tool manufacture. It is a form of cryptocrystalline quartz.

chert. A stone material made mostly of cryptocrystalline quartz, making it conducive to sharp edges. In Montana, it most commonly forms in limestone.

Clovis. One of the earliest cultures in the Americas (around 11,000 years ago), named after Clovis, New Mexico, where it was first identified.

component. A discrete period of occupation at an archaeology site.

dacite. A silica-rich volcanic rock, similar to andesite.

debitage. The waste debris generated during the manufacture of a stone tool.

drive line. Two parallel or converging lines of rocks used to help funnel bison toward bison jumps.

earth lodge. A house composed of a timber structure and earth, or sod, roof. Used during the Late Prehistoric period along the upper Missouri River.

flaking. Removal of debitage during stone tool manufacture.

flint. Synonymous with chert. Often used to describe darker varieties of chert.

flintknapping. Stone tool manufacture.

fluted. Describes a projectile point with a flake removed from the center of the base parallel to its lateral margins; unique to Clovis and Folsom cultures of the Great Plains.

Folsom. A Paleoindian culture of the Great Plains between 10,900 and 10,200 years ago.

Folsom point. A form of projectile point used during the Folsom period. Most commonly fluted, although unfluted varieties were used as well.

foreshaft. Part of an atlatl; the projectile point was hafted to the foreshaft, and the foreshaft fit into the main dart shaft.

Goshen. A Paleoindian culture of the northern Great Plains that existed around the same time as Clovis and Folsom. Goshen projectile points were not fluted, however.

graver. A small stone tool used to engrave lines or other symbols onto wood, antler, or bone. Gravers may be handheld or hafted into small handles.

grinding stone. A large rock with a flat surface upon which to prepare foods, including seeds, berries, roots, and meat.

hearth. A fire pit. It is the most common feature found at archaeology sites in Montana and was used for cooking food or providing heat.

hunter-gatherer. A person who makes a living by hunting and gathering their food.

kill site. A location where a hunter-gatherer killed and butchered an animal for food.

lanceolate point. A lance-shaped projectile point common to the Paleoindian period from 11,000 to 8,000 years ago. They are long, wide, and thin, with straight or concave bases and gently tapering lateral margins. Clovis, Goshen, and Folsom points are types of lanceolate points.

megafauna. Large animals common to the Pleistocene geologic epoch. More than thirty species of large animals went extinct in North America approximately 10,800 years ago. Today, elephants in Africa are an example of megafauna.

obsidian. A high-quality volcanic glass used throughout the world for stone tool manufacture. It is the sharpest natural material known.

occupation. A specific time period when people lived at an archaeological site. Sites often feature multiple occupations.

ochre. A soft iron oxide mineral used by Montana Native Americans as a pigment (usually red, but sometimes other colors). Commonly used in rock art and sometimes found coating artifacts and associated with burials.

peat. Decomposed plant material common in wetlands.

peck. The process of creating a petroglyph by using a sharp pointed rock to repeatedly hit the surface, producing small pits.

petroglyph. A picture pecked into the face of a rock wall, boulder, or cliff.

pictograph. A picture painted on the face of a rock, boulder, or cliff.

pit house. A human shelter constructed of timber or other plant material over an excavated circular to semicircular pit.

Pleistocene. The geologic epoch between 2 million and 11,000 years ago.

porcellanite. A dense form of chert (usually gray, black, or red) commonly found in coal formations in Montana and Wyoming.

post mold. The archaeological evidence of posts; usually holes within which posts were placed to support houses or other structures.

preform. A stone tool in its early stages of manufacture.

pressure flaker. A handheld bone, wood, or antler tool used to remove small pieces of debitage in the final steps of stone tool manufacture.

processing site. Location where a resource (stone, animal, or plant) was processed in preparation for later consumption or use.

projectile. A thrown object. In Montana, projectiles were usually spear or arrow points made of stone and used to kill animals for food.

quarry. A location where stone was obtained for making tools.

quartzite. A metamorphic rock composed of quartz sandstone; often used in stone tool manufacture in Montana.

radiocarbon. The radioactive isotope of carbon. It decays at a fixed rate that can be measured to determine the date of an organism's death.

rhyolite. A fine-grained, silica-rich volcanic rock often used throughout the world for stone tool manufacture, but not common in Montana.

scraper. A stone tool used to scrape hides for preparation as clothing. Scrapers may be handheld or hafted onto handles.

sherds. Small pieces of broken pottery found at archaeological sites.

silica. Silicon dioxide. Glass, quartz, chert, and obsidian are all composed of this chemical substance.

silicified. Describes a natural material that has been replaced with silica over many thousands of years; silicified materials are glassy due to their high silica content and were often used in stone tool production.

stone circle. A ring of rocks found at archaeological sites in the Great Plains. Most often interpreted as the remains of tepee structures, in which the stones were used to weigh down the hide covers.

stratigraphy. The order and position of layers of soils, artifacts, and materials at archaeological sites. Older layers are deeper (near the bottom) in the stratigraphy than more recent layers.

subsistence. Obtaining food by hunting, gathering, or agriculture.

uniface. Describes a stone tool with debitage removed from only one side, usually to form a cutting or scraping edge.

wickiup. A house structure used most commonly by the Shoshone in Montana. Composed of long timbers placed in a tepeelike structure with matting placed atop the structure to provide temporary shelter for nomadic hunter-gatherers.

References

Aaberg, Stephen A. 1985. County Line (24MO197): A Warex/Avonlea Phase Site on the Blackfoot River near Its Confluence with the Clearwater River, Missoula County, Montana. *Archaeology in Montana* 26 (1): 52–71.

Adams, Jacob, D. MacDonald, and R. Hughes. 2011. Prehistoric Lithic Raw Material Use in the Gardiner Basin, Montana. In *Yellowstone Archaeology: Northern Yellowstone*, edited by D. MacDonald and E. Hale, pp. 98–106. University of Montana Contributions to Anthropology Vol. 13, No. 1, Missoula.

Agenbroad, Larry D. 1978. *The Hudson-Meng Site: An Alberta Bison Kill in the Nebraska High Plains.* The Caxton Printers, Caldwell, Idaho.

Ahler, Stanley A. 1986. *The Knife River Flint Quarries: Excavations at Site 32DU508.* North Dakota State Historical Society, Bismarck.

Ahler, Stanley A., and Phil R. Geib. 2000. Why Flute? Folsom Point Design and Adaptation. *Journal of Archaeological Science* 27:799–820.

———. 2002. Why the Folsom Point Was Fluted: Implications from a Particular Technofunctional Explanation. In *Folsom Technology and Lifeways*, edited by John E. Clark and Michael B. Collins, pp. 371–90. Lithic Technology Special Publication Vol. 4. Department of Anthropology, University of Tulsa.

Ahler, Stanley A., T. D. Thiessen, and M. K. Trimble. 1991. *People of the Willows: The Prehistory and Early History of the Hidatsa Indians.* University of North Dakota Press, Grand Forks.

Akerman, Kim, and John L. Fagan. 1986. Fluting the Lindenmeier Folsom: A Simple and Economical Solution to the Problem, and Its Implications for Other Fluted Point Technologies. *Lithic Technology* 15 (1): 1–8.

Amick, Daniel S. 1996. Regional Patterns of Folsom Mobility and Land Use in the American Southwest. *World Archaeology* 27:411–26.

Amick, Daniel S. 1999. *Folsom Lithic Technology: Explorations in Structure and Variation.* International Monographs in Prehistory, Archaeological Series Vol. 12. Ann Arbor, Michigan.

Andrefsky, William. 1998. *Lithics.* Cambridge University Press, New York.

Antevs, Ernst. 1953. Geochronology of the Deglacial and Neothermal Ages. *Journal of Geology* 61 (3): 195–230.

Armstrong, Steven. 1993. Alder Complex Kitchens: Experimental Replication of Paleoindian Cooking Facilities. *Archaeology in Montana* 34 (2): 1–67.

Arthur, George W. 1966. *An Archaeological Survey of the Upper Yellowstone River Drainage, Montana.* Agricultural Economics Research Report No. 26, Bozeman, Montana.

Bamforth, Douglas B. 1991. Flintknapping Skill, Communal Hunting, and Paleoindian Projectile Point Typology. *Plains Anthropologist* 36:309–22.

———. 2002. High-Tech Foragers? Folsom and Later Paleoindian Technology on the Great Plains. *Journal of World Prehistory* 16:55–98.

Bamforth, Douglas B., and Peter Bleed. 1997. Technology, Flaked Stone Technology, and Risk. In *Rediscovering Darwin: Evolutionary Theory in Archeological Explanation,* edited by C. Michael Barton and Geoffrey A. Clark, pp. 109–40. Archeological Papers of the American Anthropological Association Vol. 7. Arlington, Virginia.

Barsh, R. L., and C. Marlor. 2003. Driving Bison and Blackfoot Science. *Human Ecology* 31 (4): 571–93.

Baughton, John. 2005. *Phase I Survey and Inventory of the Eyebrow Archaeological Site.* Report on file at the Bureau of Land Management Office, Missoula, Montana.

Baumler, Mark F. 1997. A Little Down the Trail: Prehistoric Obsidian Use on the Flying D Ranch, Northern Gallatin-Madison River Divide, Southwestern Montana. *Tebiwa* 26 (2): 141–61.

———. 2008. Assault on Basalt: The Cashman Quarry Site. *Montana: The Magazine of Western History* 58 (2): 74–75.

Baumler, Mark F., C. G. Helm, S. Platt, P. Rennie, and S. Wilmoth. 2001. Assault on Basalt: The Cashman Quarry Site, Madison County, Southwestern Montana. *Archaeology in Montana* 42 (2): 1–26.

Berry, Derek S. 2006. Data Recovery Efforts at Site 24DL470, Deer Lodge County, Montana. *Archaeology in Montana* 48 (2): 1–19.

Boldurian, Anthony T., Philip T. Fitzgibbons, and Phillip H. Shelley. 1985. Fluting Devices in the Folsom Tradition: Patterning in Debitage Formation and Projectile Point Basal Configuration. *Plains Anthropologist* 30:293–304.

Bonnichsen, R., M. Beatty, M. Turner, J. Turner, and D. Douglas. 1992. Paleoindian Lithic Procurement at the South Fork of Everson Creek, Southwestern Montana: A Preliminary Statement. In *Ice Age Hunters of the Rockies,* edited by D. J. Stanford and J. S. Day, pp. 285–322. University Press of Colorado, Boulder.

Bonnichsen, Robson, and Karen L. Turnmire (editors). 1991. *Clovis: Origins and Adaptations*. Center for the Study of the First Americans, Oregon State University, Corvallis.

Bradley, Bruce A. 1982. Flaked Stone Technology and Typology. In *The Agate Basin Site*, edited by G. Frison and D. Stanford, pp. 181–212. Academic Press, New York.

———. 1993. Paleo-Indian Flaked Stone Technology in the North American High Plains. In *From Kostenki to Clovis*, edited by O. Soffer and N. D. Praslov, pp. 251–62. Plenum Press, New York.

Brink, Jack W. 2008. *Imagining Head-Smashed-In*. Athabasca University Press, Edmonton, Alberta.

Brumley, John H. 1975. *The Cactus Flower Site in Southeastern Alberta: 1972–1974 Excavations*. National Museum of Man Series, Archaeological Survey of Canada Paper No. 46, Ottawa, Ontario.

———. 1975. Radiocarbon Dates from the Wahkpa Chu'gn Site. *Archaeology in Montana* 16 (2–3): 105–16.

———. 1976. *The Wahkpa Chu'gn Archaeological Site*. H. Earl Clack Museum, Havre, Montana.

Bryan, Liz. 2005. *The Buffalo People: Pre-Contact Archaeology on the Canadian Plains*. Heritage House, Surrey, British Columbia.

Buchanan, Briggs, and Mark Collard. 2008. Phenetics, Cladistics, and the Search for the Alaskan Ancestors of the Paleoindians: A Reassessment of Relationships among the Clovis, Nenana, and Denali Archaeological Complexes. *Journal of Archaeological Science* 35:1683–94.

Church, Tim. 1994. *Lithic Resource Studies: A Sourcebook for Archaeologists*. Lithic Technology Special Publication No. 3, Department of Anthropology, University of Tulsa.

———. 1996. Lithic Resources of the Bearlodge Mountains, Wyoming: Description, Distribution, and Implications. *Plains Anthropologist* 41 (156): 135–64.

Clark, Frances. 1984. Knife River Flint and Interregional Exchange. *Midcontinental Journal of Archaeology* 9:173–98.

Clark, John E., and Michael B. Collins (editors). 2002. *Folsom Technology and Lifeways*. Lithic Technology Special Publication No. 4. Department of Anthropology, University of Tulsa.

Clayton, Lee, W. B. Bickley Jr., and W. J. Stone. 1970. Knife River Flint. *Plains Anthropologist* 15 (50): 282–90.

Davis, Leslie B. 1976. The Dodge Site (24RB1225): A McKean Phase Lithic Cache in the Tongue River Valley. *Archaeology in Montana* 17 (1–2): 35–51.

———. 1978. The 20th-Century Commercial Mining of Northern Plains Bison Kills. In *Bison Procurement and Utilization*, edited by L. B. Davis and M. Wilson, pp. 254–86. *Plains Anthropologist* Memoir 14.

———. 1981. *Cattleguard No. 3: Intensive Small-Scale Mitigation Excavations at the South Everson Creek Chert Quarry/Workshop Site (24BE559) in Southwestern Montana*. Report on file at the Bureau of Land Management, Dillon, Montana.

———. 1982. Montana Archaeology and Radiocarbon Chronology, 1962–1981. *Archaeology of Montana*, Special Issue 3.

———. 1982. Schmitt Chert Quarries. Unpublished manuscript on file at Museum of the Rockies, Bozeman, Montana.

———. 1993. Paleo-Indian Archaeology in the High Plains and Rocky Mountains of Montana. In *From Kostenki to Clovis*, edited by O. Soffer and N. D. Praslov, pp. 263–77. Plenum Press, New York.

Davis, Leslie B., Stephen A. Aaberg, James G. Schmitt, and Ann M. Johnson. 1995. *The Obsidian Cliff Plateau Prehistoric Lithic Source, Yellowstone National Park, Wyoming*. Selections from the Division of Cultural Resources No. 6, Rocky Mountain Region, National Park Service, Denver.

Davis, Leslie B., John P. Albanese, and Matthew J. Root. 2008. Hell Gap Occupation of Uplands in Lower Yellowstone Badland Country. *Archaeology in Montana* 49 (2): 51–86.

Davis, Leslie B., and Sally T. Greiser. 1992. Indian Creek Paleoindians: Early Occupation of the Elkhorn Mountains' Southeast Flank, West-Central Montana. In *Ice Age Hunters of the Rockies*, edited by D. J. Stanford and J. S. Day, pp. 225–84. University Press of Colorado, Boulder.

Davis, Leslie B., C. L. Hill, and J. W. Fisher, Jr. 2002. Radiocarbon Dates for Paleoindian Components (Folsom, Scottsbluff) at the MacHaffie Site, West-Central Montana Rockies. *Current Research in the Pleistocene* 19:18–21.

Davis, Leslie B. and E. Stallcop. 1966. The Wahkpa Chu'gn Site (24HL101): Late Hunters in the Milk River Valley, Montana. *Archaeology in Montana* Memoir 3.

Davis, Leslie B. and Charles D. Zeier. 1978. Multi-Phase Late Period Bison Procurement at the Antonsen Site, Southwestern Montana. In *Bison Procurement and Utilization*, edited by L. B. Davis and M. Wilson, pp. 222–35. *Plains Anthropologist* Memoir 14.

Dean, Walter E. 1996. Regional Aridity in North America during the Middle Holocene. *Holocene* 6 (2): 145–55.

DeBoer, Warren R. 2004. Little Bighorn on the Scioto: The Rocky Mountain Connection to Ohio Hopewell. *American Antiquity* 69 (1): 85–107.

DeMallie, Raymond J. (editor). 2001. *Handbook of the North American Indians, Volume 13: Plains*. Smithsonian Institution, Washington, D.C.

Dillehay, Tom. 1996. *Monte Verde: A Late Pleistocene Settlement in Chile, Volume 2*. Smithsonian Institution, Washington, D.C.

Duke, Philip. 1991. *Points in Time: Structure and Event in a Late Northern Plains Hunting Society*. University Press of Colorado, Boulder.

Ellis, Christopher, and James H. Payne. 1995. Estimation of Failure Rates in Fluting Based on Archaeological Data: Examples from NE North America. *Journal of Field Archaeology* 22:459–74.

Faught, Michael K. 2008. Archaeological Roots of Human Diversity in the New World: A Compilation of Accurate and Precise Radiocarbon Ages from Earliest Sites. *American Antiquity* 73 (4): 670–98.

Fiedel, Stuart J. 1999. Older Than We Thought: Implications of Corrected Dates for Paleoindians. *American Antiquity* 64:95–116.

Figgins, Jesse D. 1927. The Antiquity of Man in America. *Natural History* 27:229–39.

Firestone, R. B., A. West, J. P. Kennett, L. Becker, T. E. Bunch, Z. S. Revay, P. H. Schultz, T. Belgya, D. J. Kennett, J. M. Erlandson, O. J. Dickenson, A. C. Goodyear, R. S. Harris, G. A. Howard, J. B. Kloosterman, P. Lechler, P. A. Mayewski, J. Montgomery, R. Poreda, T. Darrah, S. S. Que Hee, A. R. Smith, A. Stich, W. Topping, J. H. Wittke, and W. S. Wolbach. 2007. Evidence for an Extraterrestrial Impact 12,900 Years Ago That Contributed to the Megafaunal Extinctions and the Younger Dryas Cooling. *Proceedings of the National Academy of Sciences* 104 (41): 16016–21.

Fisher, John W., Jr. 1995. Analysis of Archaeological Materials from Ulm Pishkun Bison Kill (24CA1012). Report submitted by Montana State University to Montana Fish, Wildlife and Parks.

———. 1995. 1995 Excavations at Ulm Pishkun Bison Kill (24CA1012). Report submitted by Montana State University to Montana Fish, Wildlife and Parks.

Fisher, John W., Jr., and Thomas E. Roll. 1999. Prehistoric Human Exploitation of Bison in the Great Plains of Montana (U.S.A.) During the Last 3,000 Years. In *Le Bison: Gibier et Moyen de Subsistance des Hommes du Paléolithique aux Paléoindiens des Grandes Plains*, edited by Jacques Jaubert and Jean-Philip Brugal, pp. 417–36. Éditions APDCA, Antibes, France.

Flenniken, J. Jeffrey. 1978. Reevaluation of the Lindenmeier Folsom: A Replication Experiment in Lithic Technology. *American Antiquity* 43:473–480.

Foor, Thomas A. 1973. The Montana Statewide Archaeological Data Retrieval System (MADS). *Archaeology in Montana* 14 (2): 44–48.

————. 1982. Cultural Continuity on the Northwestern Great Plains, 1300 B.C. to A.D. 200—the Pelican Lake Culture. Unpublished doctoral dissertation, University of California, Santa Barbara.

————. 2002. Foreword. In *The Archaeology of Mummy Cave, Wyoming: An Introduction to Shoshonean Prehistory*, edited by W. Husted and R. Edgar. National Park Service, Technical Reports Series No. 9. Midwest Archaeological Center, Lincoln, Nebraska.

Forbis, Richard G. 1960. The Old Women's Buffalo Jump, Alberta. *National Museum of Canada Bulletin* 180 (1): 56–123.

Forbis, Richard G., and John D. Sperry. 1952. An Early Man Site in Montana. *American Antiquity* 18 (2): 127–33.

Fosha, Michael. 2001. The Licking Bison Site (39HN570): An Early Archaic Bison Kill in Northwest South Dakota. *South Dakota Archaeological Society Newsletter* 31 (3–4): 1–5.

Fredlund, Dale E. 1976. Fort Union Porcellanite and Glass: Distinctive Lithic Materials of Coal Burn Origin on the Northern Plains. *Plains Anthropologist* 21 (73): 207–11.

Frison, George C. 1962. Wedding of the Waters Cave, a Stratified Site in the Big Horn Basin of Northern Wyoming. *Plains Anthropologist* 7 (18): 246–65.

————. 1965. Spring Creek Cave, Wyoming. *American Antiquity* 31 (1): 81–94.

————. 1968. A Functional Analysis of Certain Chipped Stone Tools. *American Antiquity* 33 (2): 146–55.

————. 1970. The Kobold Site, 24BH406: A Post-Altithermal Record of Buffalo Jumping for the Northwest Plains. *Plains Anthropologist* 15 (47): 1–35.

————. 1970. The Glenrock Buffalo Jump, 48CO304: Late Prehistoric Buffalo Procurement and Butchering. *Plains Anthropologist* Memoir 7.

————. 1971. The Buffalo Pound in Northwestern Plains Prehistory: Site 48 CA 302, Wyoming. *American Antiquity* 36 (1): 77–91.

————. 1974. *The Casper Site*. Academic Press, New York.

————. 1982. The Folsom Components. In *The Agate Basin Site*, edited by George C. Frison and Dennis J. Stanford, pp. 37–75. Academic Press, New York.

————. 1984. The Carter/Kerr-McGee Paleoindian Site: Cultural Resource Management and Archaeological Research. *American Antiquity* 49 (2): 288–314.

————. 1987. The University of Wyoming Investigations at the Horner Site. In *The Horner Site: The Type Site of the Cody Cultural Complex*, edited by George C. Frison and Lawrence Todd, pp. 93–106. Academic Press, New York.

———. 1991. *Prehistoric Hunters of the High Plains*. 2nd ed. Academic Press, New York.

———. 1996. *The Mill Iron Site*. University of New Mexico Press, Albuquerque.

———. 1998. The Northwestern and Northern Plains Archaic. In *Archaeology on the Great Plains*, edited by W. Raymond Wood, pp. 140–72. University Press of Kansas, Lawrence.

———. 2001. Hunting and Gathering Tradition: Northwestern and Central Plains. In *Handbook of the North American Indians, Volume 13: Plains*, edited by Raymond J. DeMallie, pp. 131–45. Smithsonian Institution, Washington D.C.

———. 2004. *Survival by Hunting*. University of California Press, Berkeley.

———. 2007. Archaic, Late Prehistoric and Early Historic Occupations. In *Medicine Lodge Creek*, edited by G. C. Frison and D. N. Walker, pp. 33–68. Clovis Press, Albuquerque, New Mexico.

———. 2007. Paleoindian Occupations. In *Medicine Lodge Creek*, edited by G. C. Frison and D. W. Walker, pp. 69–90. Clovis Press, Albuquerque, New Mexico.

Frison, George C., and Danny W. Walker. 2007. The Medicine Lodge Creek Archaeological Project. In *Medicine Lodge Creek*, edited by G. C. Frison and D. W. Walker, pp. 11–32. Clovis Press, Albuquerque, New Mexico.

Frison, George C., and Danny Walker (editors). 2007. *Medicine Lodge Creek: Holocene Archaeology of the Eastern Big Horn Basin, Wyoming*. Clovis Press, Albuquerque, New Mexico.

Frison, George C., M. Wilson, and Diane J. Wilson. 1976. Fossil Bison and Artifacts from an Early Altithermal Period Arroyo Trap in Wyoming. *American Antiquity* 41 (1): 28–57.

Galvin, Mary E. 2007. Vegetative Ecology. In *Medicine Lodge Creek*, edited by G. C. Frison and D. N. Walker, pp. 155–76. Clovis Press.

Geib, Phil R., and Stanley A. Ahler. 2002. Considerations in Folsom Fluting and Evaluation of Hand Held Indirect Percussion. In *Folsom Technology and Lifeways*, edited by John E. Clark and Michael B. Collins, pp. 249–72. Lithic Technology Special Publication No. 4. Dept. of Anthropology, University of Tulsa.

Gilbert, M. Thomas P, Dennis L. Jenkins, Anders Gotherstrom, Nuria Naveran, Juan J. Sanchez, Michael Hofreiter, Philip Francis Thomsen, Jonas Binladen, Thomas F. G. Higham, Robert M. Yohe II, Robert

Parr, Linda Scott Cummings, and Eske Willerslev. 2008. DNA from Pre-Clovis Human Coprolites in Oregon, North America. *Science* 320 (5877): 786–89.

Gillespie, Jason D. 2007. Enculturing an Unknown World: Caches and Clovis Landscape Ideology. *Canadian Journal of Archaeology* 31 (2): 171–89.

Gilmore, Melvin R. 1977. *Uses of Plants by the Indians of the Missouri River Region*. University of Nebraska Press, Lincoln.

Goebel, Ted, Michael R. Waters, and Dennis H. O'Rourke. 2008. The Late Pleistocene Dispersal of Modern Humans in the Americas. *Science* 319 (5869): 1497–1502.

Grayson, Donald K., and David J. Meltzer. 2003. A Requiem for North American Overkill. *Journal of Archaeological Science* 30:585–93.

Gregg, Michael L. 1985. *An Overview of the Prehistory of Western and Central North Dakota*. Bureau of Land Management Cultural Resource Series No. 1, Billings, Montana.

Greiser, Sally T. 1994. Late Prehistoric Cultures on the Montana Plains. In *Plains Indians, A.D. 500–1500: The Archaeological Past of Historic Groups*, edited by Karl H. Schlesier, pp. 34–55. University of Oklahoma Press, Norman.

Greiser, Sally T., T. Weber Greiser, and Susan M. Vetter. 1985. Middle Prehistoric Period Adaptations and Paleoenvironment in the Northwestern Plains: The Sun River Site. *American Antiquity* 50 (4): 849–77.

Gryba, Eugene M. 1988. A Stone Age Pressure Method of Folsom Fluting. *Plains Anthropologist* 33 (119): 53–66.

Haines, A. L. 1966. The Rigler Bluffs Hearth Site: 24PA401. *Archaeology in Montana* 7 (2): 5.

Hale, Elaine S. 2003. A Culture History of the Yellowstone River and Yellowstone Lake, Yellowstone National Park, Wyoming and Montana. Master's thesis, University of Montana, Missoula.

Hamilton, Joseph S. 2007. The Tongue River Bison Jump (24RB2135): The Technological Organization of Late Prehistoric Period Hunter-Gatherers in Southeastern Montana. Master's thesis, University of Montana, Missoula.

Harris, Arthur H. 2002. The Mummy Cave Tetrapods. In *The Archaeology of Mummy Cave, Wyoming: An Introduction to Shoshonean Prehistory*, pp. 163–70, edited by W. Husted and R. Edgar. National Park Service, Technical Reports Series No. 9. Midwest Archaeological Center, Lincoln, Nebraska.

Haspel, Howard H., Tom Lessard, Alan Wimer, and Marcel Kornfeld. 1995. Analysis of Selected McKean Site Artifacts. In *Keyhole Reservoir Archaeology: Glimpses of the Past from Northeast Wyoming*, edited by M. Kornfeld, G. C. Frison, and M. L. Larson, pp. 273–86. Occasional Papers on Wyoming Archaeology No. 5, Office of the Wyoming State Archaeologist, Laramie.

Hayden, Brian. 1982. Interaction Parameters and the Demise of Paleo-Indian Craftsmanship. *Plains Anthropologist* 27 (96): 109–23.

Hayden, Brian, and Rick Schulting. 1997. The Plateau Interaction Sphere and Late Prehistoric Cultural Complexity. *American Antiquity* 62 (1): 51–85.

Haynes, C. Vance, Jr. 1993. Clovis-Folsom Geochronology and Climatic Change. In *From Kostenki to Clovis*, edited by O. Soffer and N. D. Praslov, pp. 9–45. Plenum Press, New York.

———. 2008. Younger Dryas "Black Mats" and the Rancholabrean Termination in North America. *Proceedings of the National Academy of Sciences* 105 (18): 6520–25.

Haynes, C. Vance, Jr., Roelf P. Beukens, A. J. T. Jull, and Owen K. Davis. 1992. New Radiocarbon Dates for Some Old Folsom Sites: Accelerator Technology. In *Ice Age Hunters of the Rockies*, edited by D. J. Stanford and J. S. Day, pp. 83–100. University Press of Colorado, Boulder.

Haynes, C. Vance, Jr., Marcel Kornfeld, and G. C. Frison. 2004. New Geochronological and Archaeological Data for the Sheaman Clovis Site, Eastern Wyoming, U.S.A. *Geoarchaeology* 19 (4): 369–79.

Herbel, Brian, Todd Ahlman, Eric Carlson, and Shari Silverman. 2010. *Data Recovery at Sites 24LN202 and 24LN2210, Libby to Bonners Ferry Transmission Line Rebuild Project, Lincoln County, Montana.* Report submitted by HRA, Inc., to Bonneville Power Administration.

Hill, Matthew E., Jr. 2007. A Moveable Feast: Variation in Faunal Resource Use among Central and Western North American Paleoindian Sites. *American Antiquity* 72 (3): 417–38.

———. 2008. Variation in Paleoindian Fauna Use on the Great Plains and Rocky Mountains of North America. *Quaternary International* 191:34–52.

Hofman, Jack L. 1994. Paleoindian Aggregations on the Great Plains. *Journal of Anthropological Archaeology* 13 (4): 341–70.

Hughes, Susan S. 1991. Division of Labor at a Besant Hunting Camp in Eastern Montana. *Plains Anthropologist* 36 (134): 25–49.

Hunzicker, David A. 2008. Folsom Projectile Technology: An Experiment in Design, Effectiveness, and Efficiency. *Plains Anthropologist* 53 (3): 291–311.

Husted, Wilfred M. 1995. The Western Macrotradition Twenty-Seven Years Later. *Archaeology in Montana* 36 (1): 37–92.

Husted, Wilfred M., and Robert Edgar. 2002. *The Archaeology of Mummy Cave, Wyoming: An Introduction to Shoshonean Prehistory*. National Park Service, Technical Reports Series No. 9. Midwest Archaeological Center, Lincoln, Nebraska.

Ingbar, Eric E. 1992. The Hanson Site and Folsom on the Northwestern Plains. In *Ice Age Hunters of the Rockies*, edited by D. J. Stanford and J. S. Day, pp. 169–92. University Press of Colorado, Boulder.

Ingbar, Eric E. and Jack L. Hofman. 1999. Folsom Fluting Fallacies. In *Folsom Lithic Technology*, edited by Daniel S. Amick, pp. 98–110. International Monographs in Prehistory, Archaeological Series Vol. 12. Ann Arbor, Michigan.

Irwin-Williams, C., H. Irwin, G. Agogino, and C. V. Haynes. 1973. Hell Gap: Paleo-Indian Occupation on the High Plains. *Plains Anthropologist* 18 (59): 40–53.

Jodry, M. A., and D. J. Stanford. 1992. Stewart's Cattle Guard Site: An Analysis of Bison Remains in a Folsom Bison Kill–Butchery Campsite. In *Ice-Age Hunters of the Rockies*, edited by D. J. Stanford and J. S. Day, pp. 101–68. University Press of Colorado, Boulder.

Johnson, Ann M. 1988. Parallel Grooved Ceramics: An Addition to Avonlea Material Culture. In *Avonlea Yesterday and Today: Archaeology and Prehistory*, edited by L. B. Davis, pp. 137–43. Saskatchewan Archaeological Society, Saskatoon.

Johnson, Ann M., and Alfred E. Johnson. 1998. The Plains Woodland. In *Archaeology on the Great Plains*, pp. 201–34, edited by W. Raymond Wood. University Press of Kansas, Lawrence.

Johnson, Ann M., Brian Reeves, and Mack Shortt. 2004. *The Osprey Beach (Site 48YE409/410), Yellowstone National Park, Wyoming*. Report on file at the Yellowstone Center for Resources, Yellowstone National Park, Mammoth Hot Springs, Wyoming.

Jones, Terry L., J. F. Porcasi, J. M. Erlandson, H. Dallas Jr., T. A. Wake, and R. Schwaderer. 2008. The Protracted Holocene Extinction of California's Flightless Sea Duck (*Chendytes lawi*) and Its Implications for the Pleistocene Overkill Hypothesis. *Proceedings of the National Academy of Sciences* 105:4105–4108.

Judge, W. James. 1970. Systems Analysis and the Folsom-Midland Question. *Southwestern Journal of Anthropology* 26 (1): 40–51.

Kehoe, Thomas F. 1963. Book Review: *The Old Women's Buffalo Jump, Alberta* by Richard G. Forbis. *American Antiquity* 28 (4): 561–62.

———. 1966. The Small Side-Notched Point System of the Northern Plains. *American Antiquity* 31 (6): 827–41.

———. 1967. The Boarding School Bison Drive Site. *Plains Anthropologist* Memoir 4.

Kennett, D. J. J. P. Kennett, A. West, C. Mercer, S. S. Que Hee, L. Bement, T. E. Bunch, M. Sellers, and W. S. Wolbach. 2009. Nanodiamonds in the Younger Dryas Boundary Sediment Layer. *Science* 323 (5910): 94.

Keyser, James D., and Carl M. Davis. 1984. Lightning Spring: 4,000 Years of Pine Parkland Prehistory. *Archaeology in Montana* 25 (2–3): 1–64.

Keyser, James D., and John L. Fagan. 1993. McKean Lithic Technology at Lightning Spring. *Plains Anthropologist* 38 (145): 37–51.

Keyser, James D., and Michael A. Klassen. 2001. *Plains Indian Rock Art*. University of Washington Press, Seattle.

Keyser, James D., and James R. Wettstaed. 1995. Lightning Strikes Again: Excavation of Additional McKean Levels at the Lightning Spring Site (39HN204). *Archaeology in Montana* 36 (1): 1–32.

Kinney, W. Jeffrey. 1996. The Hagen Site, 24DW1: A Review of Historical Data and Reassessment of Its Ceramic Assemblage and Position in Northern Plains Prehistory. Master's thesis, University of Montana, Missoula.

Kinsner, John J. 2010. *Paleoindian Land Use in Glacier National Park*. Report prepared for Glacier National Park, West Glacier, Montana.

Knudson, Ruthann. 1983. Organizational Variability in Late Paleoindian Assemblages. PhD dissertation, Washington State University, Pullman.

Kooyman, B., L. V. Hills, P. McNeil, and S. Tolman. 2006. Late Pleistocene Horse Hunting at the Wally's Beach Site (DhPg-8), Canada. *American Antiquity* 71 (1): 101–21.

Kooyman, B., M. E. Newman, C. Cluney, M. Lobb, S. Tolman, P. McNeil, and L. V. Hills. 2001. Identification of Horse Exploitation by Clovis Hunters Based on Protein Analysis. *American Antiquity* 66 (4): 686–91.

Kornfeld, Marcel. 1995. Chronology and Occupational Continuity of the McKean Site. In *Keyhole Reservoir Archaeology: Glimpses of the Past from Northeast Wyoming*, edited by M. Kornfeld, G. C. Frison, and M. L. Larson, pp. 267–85. Occasional Papers on Wyoming Archaeology No. 5, Office of the Wyoming State Archaeologist, Laramie.

Kornfeld, Marcel, Kaoru Akoshima, and G. C. Frison. 1990. Stone Tool Caching on the North American Plains: Implications of the McKean Site Tool Kit. *Journal of Field Archaeology* 17 (3): 301–9.

Kornfeld, Marcel, G. C. Frison, M. L. Larson, J. C. Miller, and J. Saysette. 1999. Paleoindian Bison Procurement and Paleoenvironments in Middle Park of Colorado. *Geoarchaeology* 14:655–674.

Kornfeld Marcel, Michael Harkin, and J. Durr. 2001. Landscapes and the Peopling of the Americas. In *On Being First: Cultural Innovation and Environmental Consequences of First Peopling*, edited by J. Gillespie, S. Tapakka, and C. G. deMille, pp. 149–62. University of Calgary.

Kornfeld, Marcel, and M. L. Larson. 2008. Bonebeds and Other Myths: Paleoindian to Archaic Transition on North American Great Plains and Rocky Mountains. *Quaternary International* 191:18–33.

Kornfeld, Marcel, M. L. Larson, D. J. Rapson, and G. C. Frison. 2001. 10,000 Years in the Rocky Mountains: The Helen Lookingbill Site. *Journal of Field Archaeology* 28 (3–4): 307–24.

Kornfeld, Marcel, M. L. Larson, and D. N. Walker. 1995. McKean Site Testing: General Results. In *Keyhole Reservoir Archaeology: Glimpses of the Past from Northeast Wyoming*, edited by M. Kornfeld, G. C. Frison, and M. L. Larson, pp. 233–72. Occasional Papers on Wyoming Archaeology No. 5, Office of the Wyoming State Archaeologist, Laramie.

Kornfeld, Marcel, Lawrence C. Todd, Eric E. Ingbar, and David J. Rapson. 1995. Introduction to the McKean Site Testing: Field Methods and Lab Procedures. In *Keyhole Reservoir Archaeology: Glimpses of the Past from Northeast Wyoming*, edited by M. Kornfeld, G. C. Frison, and M. L. Larson, pp. 223–31. Occasional Papers on Wyoming Archaeology No. 5, Office of the Wyoming State Archaeologist, Laramie.

Lahren, Larry. 1976. The Myers-Hindman Site: An Exploratory Study of Human Occupation Patterns in the Upper Yellowstone Valley from 7000 B.C. to A.D. 1200. Master's thesis, University of Calgary.

———. 2001. The On-Going Odyssey of the Anzick Clovis Burial in Park County, Montana (24PA506): Part 1. *Archaeology in Montana* 42 (1): 55–60.

———. 2006. *Homeland: An Archaeologist's View of Yellowstone Country's Past*. Cayuse Press, Livingston, Montana.

Lahren, Larry, and Robson Bonnichsen. 1974. Bone Foreshafts from a Clovis Burial in Southwestern Montana. *Science* 186 (4159): 147–50.

Larson, Mary Lou, Marcel Kornfeld, and George C. Frison (editors). 2009. *Hell Gap: A Stratified Paleoindian Campsite at the Edge of the Rockies*. University of Utah Press, Salt Lake City.

Laughlin, John P. 2005. 149 Refits: Assessing Site Integrity and Hearth-Centered Activities at Barger Gulch Locality B. Master's thesis, University of Wyoming, Laramie.

Livers, Michael C., and Douglas H. MacDonald. 2009. *Airport Rings: Stone Circle Archaeology in Yellowstone National Park*. Report prepared for Yellowstone National Park by the University of Montana, Missoula.

Loendorf, Lawrence L., J. C. Dahlberg, and L. O. Weston. 1981. *The Pretty Creek Archaeological Site 24CB4 and 5*. Report on file at the Midwest Archaeological Center, Lincoln, Nebraska.

Loendorf, Lawrence L., D. Kuehn, and N. F. Forsman. 1984. Rainy Buttes Silicified Wood: A Source of Lithic Raw Material in Western North Dakota. *Plains Anthropologist* 29 (106): 4–20.

Low, Bruce. 1996. Swan River Chert. *Plains Anthropologist* 41 (156): 165–74.

Lyman, R. Lee. 2004. Aboriginal Overkill in the Intermountain West of North America: Zooarchaeological Tests and Implications. *Human Nature* 15:169–208.

MacDonald, Douglas H. 1998. Subsistence, Sex, and Cultural Transmission in Folsom Culture. *Journal of Anthropological Archaeology* 17 (3): 217–39.

———. 1999. Modeling Folsom Mobility, Mating Strategies, and Technological Organization in the Northern Plains. *Plains Anthropologist* 44 (168): 141–61.

———. 2008. *Final Inventory and Evaluation Report, Yellowstone National Park: 2007 Boundary Lands Archeological Survey and National Register Evaluation, Site 24YE355 Cinnabar/Yellowstone Bank Cache Site*. Report prepared for Yellowstone National Park by the University of Montana, Missoula.

———. 2009. Results of the 2009 Montana Yellowstone Archaeological Project, Yellowstone Lake, Wyoming. Paper presented at the 67th Plains Anthropology Conference, Norman, Oklahoma.

———. 2010. The Evolution of Folsom Fluting. *Plains Anthropologist* 55 (213): 39–54.

MacDonald, Douglas H., Lester E. Maas, and Jonathon Hardes. 2010. The Yellowstone Bank Cache Site (24YE355): A Late Archaic Pelican Lake Site on the Yellowstone River, Gardiner, Montana. *Archaeology in Montana* 51 (2): 1–24.

Malouf, Carling. 1961. The Tipi Rings of the High Plains. *American Antiquity* 26 (3): 381–89.

Mandryk, Carole, and H. Josenhans. 2001. Late Quaternary Paleoenvironments in Northwestern North America: Implications for Inland vs. Coastal Migration Routes. *Quaternary Science Reviews* 20:301–14.

Martin, James E., R. A. Alex, L. M. Alex, J. P. Abbott, R. C. Benton, and L. F. Miller. 1993. The Beaver Creek Shelter (39CU779): A Holocene Succession in the Black Hills of South Dakota. *Plains Anthropologist* 38 (145): 17–36.

Martin, Paul S. 2005. *Twilight of the Mammoths*. University of California Press, Berkeley.

McDonald, Jerry N. 1981. *North American Bison: Their Classification and Evolution*. University of California Press, Berkeley.

McMillan, Alan D., and Eldon Yellowhorn. 2004. *First Peoples in Canada*. Douglas and McIntyre, Vancouver, British Columbia.

Melton, Douglas A. 1988. Variation in the Artifact Assemblages from Five Oxbow Sites. Master's thesis, University of Montana, Missoula.

Meltzer, David J. 1999. Human Responses to Middle Holocene (Altithermal) Climates on the North American Great Plains. *Quaternary Research* 52:404–16.

———. 2006. *Folsom: New Archaeological Investigations of a Classic Paleoindian Bison Kill*. University of California Press, Berkeley.

Meltzer, D. J., D. K. Grayson, G. Ardila, A. W. Barker, D. F. Dincauze, C. V. Haynes, F. Mena, L. Nuñez, and D. J. Stanford. 1997. On the Pleistocene Antiquity of Monte Verde, Southern Chile. *American Antiquity* 62 (4): 659–63.

Metcalf, M. D, and S. A. Ahler (editors). 1995. *Alkali Creek: A Stratified Record of Prehistoric Flint Mining in North Dakota*. Report prepared for the USDA Soil Conservation Service by Metcalf Archaeological Consultants, Inc., Eagle, Colorado.

Morrow, Juliet E., and Toby A. Morrow. 1999. Geographic Variation in Fluted Projectile Points: A Hemispheric Perspective. *American Antiquity* 64 (2): 215–30.

Mulloy, W. T. 1942. *The Hagen Site: A Prehistoric Village on the Lower Yellowstone*. University of Montana Publications in the Social Sciences No. 1., Missoula.

———. 1954. The McKean Site in Northeastern Wyoming. *Southwestern Journal of Anthropology* 10 (4): 432–60.

———. 1958. A Preliminary Historical Outline for the Northwestern Plains. *University of Wyoming Publications* 22(1–2).

Nabokov, Peter, and Lawrence Loendorf. 2002. *American Indians and Yellowstone National Park: A Documentary Overview*. National Park Service, Yellowstone Center for Resources, Yellowstone National Park, Wyoming.

Neal, Barbara S. 2006. Precontact Utilization of Sandhill Environments during the Pelican Lake and Besant Phases. Master's thesis, University of Saskatchewan, Saskatoon.

O'Brien, Michael J., R. Lee Lyman, and Michael B. Schiffer. 2007. *Archaeology as a Process*. University of Utah Press, Salt Lake City.

Payette, Jacqueline M., Lynelle A. Peterson, and Edwin Hajic. 2006. Investigations at the Vestal Site (24FR760): An Avonlea Bison Processing Site. *Archaeology in Montana* 47 (1): 1–96.

Peterson, Lynelle M. 1999. *Cultural Investigations along the Montana Segment of the Express Pipeline: Volume 5—Investigations of the*

Buckeye Site (24CB1266), a Multi-Component Campsite near the Pryor Mountains in Southern Montana. Report on file at the Montana Historical Society, Helena.

Pierce, William G. 1963. Cathedral Cliffs Formation, the Early Acid Breccia Unit of Northwestern Wyoming. *Geological Society of America Bulletin* 74 (1): 9–22.

Prentiss, Anna M., Guy Cross, T. A. Foor, Mathew Hogan, Dirk Markle, and David S. Clarke. 2008. Evolution of a Late Prehistoric Winter Village on the Interior Plateau of British Columbia: Geophysical Investigations, Radiocarbon Dating, and Spatial Analysis of the Bridge River Site. *American Antiquity* 73 (1): 59–81.

Prentiss, Anna M., Robert C. O'Boyle, Lucille Harris, and Dylan Haymans. 2007. *Report of the 2006 University of Montana Archaeological Investigations of the East Fork Reservoir Locality (Testing of Sites 24HL465, 24HL1085, and 24HL1215; Data Recovery at 24HL1215)*. Report on file at University of Montana Department of Anthropology, Missoula.

Reeves, Brian O. K. 1973. The Concept of an Altithermal Cultural Hiatus in Northern Plains Prehistory. *American Anthropologist* 75 (5): 1221–1253.

———. 1978. Head-Smashed-In: 5500 Years of Bison Jumping in the Alberta Plains. In *Bison Procurement and Utilization*, edited by L. B. Davis and M. Wilson, pp. 151–74. *Plains Anthropologist* Memoir 14.

———. 1983. The Kenney Site: A Stratified Campsite in Southwestern Alberta. *Archaeology in Montana* 24 (1): 1–135.

———. 1983. Six Millenniums of Buffalo Kills. *Scientific American* 249 (4): 120–35.

———. 1990. Communal Bison Hunters of the Northern Plains. In *Hunters of the Recent Past*, edited by L. B. Davis and B. O. K. Reeves, pp. 169–94. Unwin Hyman, London.

———. 2003. *Mistakis: The Archeology of Waterton-Glacier International Peace Park, Archeological Inventory and Assessment Program 1993-1996 Final Technical Report*, Vol. 1 and 2. Report prepared for Glacier National Park by the University of Calgary.

Reher, Charles A. 1978. Bison Population and Other Deterministic Factors in a Model of Adaptive Process on the Shortgrass Plains. In *Bison Procurement and Utilization*, edited by L. B. Davis and M. Wilson, pp. 23–39. *Plains Anthropologist* Memoir 14.

Reher, Charles A., and G. C. Frison. 1980. The Vore Site 48CK302: A Stratified Buffalo Jump in the Wyoming Black Hills. *Plains Anthropologist* Memoir 16.

Rennie, Patrick J. 1994. The McKean Complex: An Analysis of Six Middle Prehistoric Period Sites in the Northwestern Plains. Master's thesis, University of Montana, Missoula.

Rennie, P., M. Baumler, C. Helm, R. Hughes, D. Murdo, S. Platt, and S. Wilmoth. 2008. Grady Ranch (24LC2013): A Newly Characterized Dacite Procurement Locality in West-Central Montana. *Archaeology in Montana* 49 (1): 1–14.

Roll, Tom E., Michael Neeley, Robert Speakman, and Michael Glascock. 2005. Characterization of Montana Cherts by LA-ICP-MS. In *Laser Ablation ICP-MS in Archaeological Research*, edited by R. J. Speakman, pp. 59–76. University of New Mexico Press, Albuquerque.

Root, Matthew J. 1992. The Knife River Flint Quarries: The Organization of Stone Tool Production. PhD Dissertation. University Microfilms International, Ann Arbor, Michigan.

———. 2001. Intrasite Comparisons. In *The Archaeology of the Bobtail Wolf Site*, edited by Matthew J. Root, pp. 347–62. WSU Press, Pullman, Washington.

Root, Matthew J., and Leslie B. Davis. 2006. A Possible Folsom-Midland Association in the Northern Rocky Mountains. *Current Research in the Pleistocene* 23:142–44.

Root, Matthew J., E. J. Knell, and J. Taylor. 2007. Cody Complex Land-Use in Western North Dakota and Southern Saskatchewan. Paper presented at the 65th Plains Anthropological Meeting, Rapid City, South Dakota.

Root, Matthew J., Jerry D. William, Marvin Kay, and Lisa Shifrin. 1999. Folsom Ultrathin Biface and Radial Break Tools in the Knife River Flint Quarry Area. In *Folsom Lithic Technology*, edited by Daniel S. Amick, pp. 144–68. International Monographs in Prehistory, Archaeological Series Vol. 12, Ann Arbor, Michigan.

Sanders, Paul. 2000. *The 1999 Archaeological Test Excavations of Site 24YE14, Yellowstone National Park, Wyoming*. Report on file at the National Park Service, Denver.

———. 2002. Prehistoric Land-Use Patterns within the Yellowstone Lake Basin and Hayden Valley Region, Yellowstone National Park, Wyoming. In *Proceedings of the George Wright Symposium*, pp. 213–31. George Wright Society, Hancock, Michigan.

———. 2005. *The 2003–2004 Archaeological Investigation of Sites in the Lamar River Valley and in the Black Canyon of the Yellowstone River, Yellowstone National Park*. Office of the Wyoming State Archeologist, Laramie.

Scheiber, Laura. 2006. Skeletal Biology: Plains. In *Handbook of North American Indians, Volume 3: Environment, Origins, and Population*, edited by D. H. Ubelaker, pp. 595–609. Smithsonian Institution, Washington, D.C.

Schlesier, Karl H. (editor). 1994. *Plains Indians, A.D. 500–1500: The Archaeological Past of Historic Groups*. University of Oklahoma Press, Norman.

Sellet, Frederic. 2004. Beyond the Point: Projectile Manufacture and Behavioral Inference. *Journal of Archaeological Science* 31 (11): 1553–1566.

Sellet, Frederic, James Donohue, and Matthew G. Hill. 2009. The Jim Pitts Site: A Stratified Paleoindian Site in the Black Hills of South Dakota. *American Antiquity* 74 (4): 735–758.

Shumate, Maynard. 1967. The Carter Ferry Buffalo Kill. *Archaeology in Montana* 8 (2): 1–10.

Sollberger, Jerry B. 1985. A Technique for Folsom Fluting. *Lithic Technology* 14 (1): 41–50.

Stanford, Dennis J. 1978. The Jones-Miller Site. In *Bison Procurement and Utilization*, edited by L. B. Davis and M. Wilson, pp. 90–97. *Plains Anthropologist* Memoir 14.

Stanford, Dennis, and Bruce Bradley. 2002. Ocean Trails and Prairie Paths: Thoughts about Clovis Origins. In *The First Americans: The Pleistocene Colonization of the New World*, edited by Nina G. Jablonski, pp. 255–71. Memoirs of the California Academy of Sciences No. 27, San Francisco.

Straus, Lawrence G. 2000. Solutrean Settlement of North America? A Review of Reality. *American Antiquity* 63:7–20.

Surovell, T. A., J. B. Finley, G. M. Smith, P. J. Brantingham, and R. Kelly. 2009. Correcting Temporal Frequency Distributions for Taphonomic Bias. *Journal of Archaeological Science* 36:1715–24.

Syms, Leigh. 1969. The McKean Complex as a Horizon Marker in Manitoba and on the Northern Great Plains. Master's thesis, University of Manitoba, Winnipeg.

Taylor, Dee C. 1973. *Archaeological Investigations in the Libby Reservoir Area, Northwestern Montana*. University of Montana, Missoula.

Taylor, Dee C., K. Wood and J. J. Hoffman. 1964. *Preliminary Archaeological Investigation in the Yellowstone National Park*. Montana State University, Missoula.

Taylor, R. E., C. Vance Haynes Jr., and Minze Stuiver. 1996. Clovis and Folsom Age Estimates: Stratigraphic Context and Radiocarbon Calibration. *Antiquity* 70 (269): 515–25.

Thoms, Alston V. 2006. Summary: National Register Evaluations, Land-Use Findings and Interpretations for Hunter-Gatherer and Agro-Industrial Sites. In *Sites and Site Formation Processes in the Tobacco*

Plains and Vicinity: Archaeological Investigations in the Middle Kootenai River Valley, Northwest Montana, edited by A. V. Thoms and P. A. Clabaugh, pp. 353–68. Reports of Investigations No. 9. Center for Ecological Archaeology, Texas A&M University, College Station.

Thoms, Alston V. (editor). 1984. *Volume I: Environment, Archaeology, and Land Use Patterns in the Middle Kootenai River Valley.* Center for Northwest Anthropology, Washington State University, Pullman.

Thoms, Alston V., and Greg C. Burtchard (editors). 1987. *Prehistoric Land Use in the Northern Rocky Mountains: A Perspective from the Middle Kootenai River Valley.* Center for Northwest Anthropology Project Report Number 4, Washington State University, Pullman.

Thoms, Alston V., and P. A. Clabaugh (editors). 2006. *Sites and Site Formation Processes in the Tobacco Plains and Vicinity: Archaeological Investigations in the Middle Kootenai River Valley, Northwest Montana.* Reports of Investigations No. 9. Center for Ecological Archaeology, Texas A&M University, College Station.

Thoms, Alston V., and Randall Schalk. 1985. *Cultural Resources Investigations in Libby Reservoir, Lincoln County, Northwest Montana.* Report on file at the Kootenai National Forest, Libby, Montana.

Todd, Lawrence C. 1987. Taphonomy of the Horner II Bone Bed. In *The Horner Site: The Type Site of the Cody Cultural Complex*, edited by George C. Frison and Lawrence C. Todd, pp. 107–98. Academic Press, New York.

Wagner, Jill M. 1990. The Crow-Hidatsa Schism. Master's thesis, Washington State University, Pullman.

Waguespack, Nicole M., and Todd A. Surovell. 2003. Clovis Hunting Strategies, or How to Make Out on Plentiful Resources. *American Antiquity* 68 (2): 333–52.

Walker, Danny N. 2007. Vertebrate Fauna. In *Medicine Lodge Creek*, edited by G. C. Frison and D. N. Walker, pp. 177–208. Clovis Press, Albuquerque, New Mexico.

Walker-Kuntz, Sunday A. 1999. *Cultural Investigations along the Montana Segment of the Express Pipeline, Volume 6: Investigations at the Spiro Site (24CB1332), a Middle Plains Archaic Housepit Site in Southern Alberta.* Report on file at the Montana Historical Society, Helena.

Walker-Kuntz, Sunday A., E. R. Hajic, and L. A. Peterson. 2006. The Spiro Site (24CB1332): A Middle Plains Archaic Housepit Site. *Archaeology in Montana* 47 (2): 1–56.

Waters, Michael R., and Thomas W. Stafford Jr. 2007. Redefining the Age of Clovis: Implications for the Peopling of the Americas. *Science* 315 (5815): 1122–26.

Wedel, W. R. 1961. *Prehistoric Man on the Great Plains.* University of Oklahoma Press, Norman.

Wedel, W. R., W. Husted, and J. H. Moss. 1968. Mummy Cave: Prehistoric Record from Rocky Mountains of Wyoming. *Science* 160 (3824): 184–86.

Wettlaufer, B. N. 1955. *The Mortlach Site in the Besant Valley of Central Saskatchewan.* Saskatchewan Museum of Natural History, Department of Natural Resources Anthropological Series No. 1, Regina.

Wheat, Joe Ben. 1972. The Olsen-Chubbuck Site: A Paleo-Indian Bison Kill. *Society for American Archaeology* Memoir 26. Washington, D.C.

Wilke, Philip J., J. J. Flenniken, and T. L. Ozbun. 1991. Clovis Technology at the Anzick Site, Montana. *Journal of California and Great Basin Anthropology* 13 (2): 242–72.

William, Jerry D. (editor). 2000. *The Big Black Site (32DU955C): A Folsom Complex Workshop in the Knife River Flint Quarry Area, North Dakota.* WSU Press, Pullman, Washington.

Wilmsen, Edwin N. 1974. *Lindenmeier: A Pleistocene Hunting Society.* Harper and Row, New York.

Wilmsen, Edwin N., and Frank H. H. Roberts Jr. 1979. Lindenmeier, 1934–1974: Concluding Report on Investigations. *Smithsonian Contributions to Anthropology* No. 24. Smithsonian Institution, Washington, D.C.

Wilson, Michael. 1978. Archaeological Kill Site Populations and the Holocene Evolution of the Genus *Bison.* In *Bison Procurement and Utilization,* edited by L. B. Davis and M. Wilson, pp. 9–22. *Plains Anthropologist* Memoir 14.

Winfrey, James. 1990. An Event Tree Analysis of Folsom Point Failure. *Plains Anthropologist* 35 (129): 263–72.

Winham, R. Peter, and Edward J. Lueck. 1994. Cultures of the Middle Missouri. In *Plains Indians, A.D. 500–1500: The Archaeological Past of Historic Groups,* edited by Karl H. Schlesier, pp. 149–75. University of Oklahoma Press, Norman.

Wolfe, S. A., J. Ollerhead, D. J. Huntley, and O. B. Lian. 2006. Holocene Dune Activity and Environmental Change in the Prairie Parkland and Boreal Forest, Central Saskatchewan, Canada. *Holocene* 16 (1): 17–29.

Zeier, Charles D. 1983. Besant Projectile Points from the Antonsen Site (24GA660), Gallatin County, Montana. *Archaeology in Montana* 24 (2): 1–57.

Zeimens, George M. 1981. Analysis of Postcranial Bison Remains. In *The Agate Basin Site,* edited by George C. Frison and Dennis J. Stanford, pp. 213–39. Academic Press, New York.

Zimmerman, Larry J., and Lawrence E. Bradley. 1993. The Crow Creek Massacre: Initial Coalescent Warfare and Speculations about the Genesis of Extended Coalescent. *Plains Anthropologist* Memoir 27, 38 (145): 215–26.

Index

Page numbers in italics refer to photographs.

biscuitroot, 15, 16, 67
bison, 17, 18, *20*, 75; age of, 144, 147; hunting of, 5, 19, 97–98, 123; season of, 141; spiritual importance of, 22; trade, 98; use of, 22; worn teeth of, 59. *See also* bones, beds of; buffalo jumps
Bison antiquus, 3, 6, 37, 60
Bison bison, 3, 60, 74
bison jumps. *See* buffalo jumps
Bison occidentalis, 60, 69
bitterroot, 15, 16
Bitterroot River, 14
Black Bear Coulee Site, 47, 50–51, *50, 51*, 60, 66
Blackfeet, 5, 95, 113, 115, 130, 145, 151, 153, 154, 155
Blackfoot River, 14
Black Hills, 69, 89
black mat, 35
blinds, hunting, 18, *18*
blood proteins, 24, 37
Boarding School Bison Drive, 135, 145
Bobtail Wolf Site, 33, 41, 45–46
bones: assemblage of, 11, 74; beds of, 38, 49, 118, *139*, 140, 142, 143, 145, 147, 148; needle of, 69; tools of, 34, 44, 86, 88, 93, *119*, 121, *124*
Boundary Lands, 75, 145
bow and arrow, 5, 22, 23, *23*, 125–28
Bowman chert, 25, 116
Bracken Cairn Site, 102, 116
Bridger Antelope Trap, 149
Bridge River village, 136
Broken Mammoth, 32
Browning, 145
Buckeye Site, viii, 60, 67, 75, 78, 87
buffalo berries, 16, 90
Buffalo Eddy, 105
buffalo jumps, 5, 10, 19–22, *20*, 98, 113, 123; earliest in Montana, 87. *See also* specific jumps sites
burials, 35, 36

caches, 11, 34, 35, 36
Cactus Flower Site, 75, 78, 88
camas, 15, *15*, 16
camel, 34
carbon 14, 2
Carter Ferry Buffalo Jump, 102, 107

Carter/Kerr-McGee Site, 38
Cashman Quarry, 25, 26, 27
Casper Site, 47, 48
Castle Gardens, 130
cation-ratio dating, 29, 120
Ceremonial Tradition, 130, 131
chalcedony, 25, 26, 27, 116
channel flakes, 39, 41
charcoal, 2, 11, 58, 82, 83, 101, 103, 110, 138, 145
chenopodium, 107, 111, 142
cherts, 24, 25, 27, 29, 69, 110; from Madison formation, 42, 44, 110; quarries of, *28*, 98. *See also* Avon Quarry; Bowman chert; Crescent Hill Formation; Eyebrow Quarry; Knife River Flint Quarries; Lime Creek Quarry; Logan Quarry; Schmitt Quarry; South Everson Creek Quarry; Smith River quarries
Cheyenne, 151, 154, 157–58
chokecherries, 15, 16, 22, 90
chronology, human, viii, 1–2, 8
Clark Fork River, 14, 102
Clarks Fork Yellowstone River, 85
climate, 14, 38, 81; changes in, 3, *59*, 61, 74
Clovis Culture, 2, 31–37; points of, viii, *4, 36, 39*, 39
coal seam, 38
Cody Complex, 3, 52–58; points of, viii, *4, 53, 53, 55, 57*
Cody knife, 52, *53*
Colby Site, 33, 37
Columbia Plateau, 5, 136
Columbia Plateau Tradition, 104–5
component, 11
Continental Divide, 14
cordage, 90, 94, 101, 119, 121
corrals, 5, 18, 21, 56, 98, 106, 118, 139, 145, 149
Cree, 151, 156
Crescent Hill chert, 25, 27, *28*, 83, 112
crickets, 90
Crow, 5, 8, 96, 130, 132, 136, 151, 153, 154, 157; pottery of, 129, 132, *133*, 136, 149; schism with Hidatsa, 136
Crow Creek Site, 134

About the Author

Douglas MacDonald received a PhD in anthropology from Washington State University and now teaches in the Department of Anthropology at the University of Montana. He specializes in prehistoric archaeology, stone tools, and cultural resource management. As a graduate student, he traveled the Great Plains and Rockies looking for stone sources used by flintknappers in the past. While most of the year he lives in Missoula, Montana, with his wife and two kids, during summer he leads excavations at archaeological sites throughout the state and in Yellowstone National Park.